Learning Unix for Mac OS X

Related Mac OS X Titles from O'Reilly

Essentials

AppleScript in a Nutshell
Building Cocoa Applications:
  A Step-by-Step Guide
Learning Carbon
Learning Cocoa with Objective-C
Mac OS X Pocket Guide
Macintosh Troubleshooting
  Pocket Guide
REALbasic: The Definitive Guide

Missing Manuals

AppleWorks 6: The Missing
  Manual
iMovie 2: The Missing Manual
Mac OS 9: The Missing Manual
Mac OS X: The Missing Manual
Office 2001 for Macintosh:
  The Missing Manual
Office X for Macintosh:
  The Missing Manual

Unix Essentials

Using csh & tcsh
Unix in a Nutshell
Unix Power Tools
Learning GNU Emacs
Learning the vi Editor
Objective-C Pocket Reference

Related Programming

CGI Programming with Perl
Developing Java Beans™
Java™ Cookbook
Java™ in a Nutshell
Learning Java™
Learning Perl
Perl Cookbook
Perl in a Nutshell
Practical C Programming
Programming with Qt

Mac OS X Administration

Apache: The Definitive Guide
Essential System Administration
sendmail

SECOND EDITION

Learning Unix for Mac OS X

Dave Taylor and Brian Jepson

O'REILLY®

Beijing · Cambridge · Farnham · Köln · Paris · Sebastopol · Taipei · Tokyo

Learning Unix for Mac OS X, Second Edition
by Dave Taylor and Brian Jepson

Published by O'Reilly & Associates, Inc., 1005 Gravenstein Highway North,
Sebastopol, CA 95472.

O'Reilly & Associates books may be purchased for educational, business, or sales pro-
motional use. Online editions are also available for most titles (*safari.oreilly.com*). For
more information, contact our corporate/institutional sales department: (800) 998-9938
or *corporate@oreilly.com*.

Editors:	Laurie Petrycki and Nathan Torkington
Production Editor:	Jane Ellin
Cover Designer:	Emma Colby
Interior Designer:	David Futato

Printing History:

May 2002:	First Edition.
January 2003:	Second Edition.

ISBN: 0-596-00470-2
[M]   [8/03]

Table of Contents

Preface

Mac OS X (pronounced "Mac OS Ten"), the latest incarnation of the Macintosh operating system, is a radical departure from previous versions. Not only is there a whole new look and feel (dubbed "Aqua"), there are huge differences under the hood. All the old, familiar Macintosh system software has been replaced with another operating system, called Unix. Unix is a multiuser, multitasking operating system. Being multiuser means Mac OS X allows multiple users to share the same system, each having the ability to customize the desktop, create files that can be kept private from other users, and to make settings that will automatically be restored whenever that person uses the computer. Being multitasking means the computer can easily run many different applications at the same time, and that if one application crashes or hangs, the entire system doesn't need to be rebooted.

The fact that Mac OS X is Unix under the hood doesn't matter to users who simply want to use its slick graphical interface to run their applications or manage their files. But it opens up worlds of possibilities for users who want to dig a little deeper. The Unix command-line interface, which is accessible through a Mac application called the Terminal, provides an enormous amount of power for advanced users. What's more, once you've learned to use Unix in Mac OS X, you'll also be able to use the command line in other versions of Unix or the Unix-compatible Linux.

This book is designed to teach the basics of Unix to Macintosh users. We tell you how to use the command line (which Unix users refer to as "the shell") and the filesystem, as well as some of the most useful commands. Unix is a complex and powerful system, so we only scratch the surface, but we also tell you how to deepen your Unix knowledge once you're ready for more.

Mac OS X and the Unix Family of Operating Systems

The Macintosh started out with a single-tasking operating system that allowed simple switching between applications through an application called the Finder. More recent versions of Mac OS have supported multiple applications running simultaneously, but it wasn't until the landmark release of Mac OS X that true multitasking arrived in the Macintosh world. With Mac OS X, Macintosh applications run in separate memory areas. A true multiuser system that includes proper file-level security is also finally part of the Mac.

To accomplish these improvements, Mac OS X made the jump from a proprietary underlying operating environment to Unix. Mac OS X is built on top of Darwin, a version of Unix based on BSD 4.4 Lite, FreeBSD, NetBSD, and the Mach microkernel.

Unix itself was invented more than 30 years ago for scientific and professional users who wanted a very powerful and flexible OS. It has evolved since then through a remarkably circuitous path, with stops at Bell Telephone Labs, UC Berkeley, research centers in Australia and Europe, and the U.S. Department of Defense Advanced Research Projects Agency (for funding). Because Unix was designed for experts, it can be a bit overwhelming at first. But after you get the basics (from this book!) you'll start to appreciate some of the reasons to use Unix:

- It comes with a huge number of powerful application programs. You can get many others for free on the Internet. (The Fink project, available from SourceForge (*http://fink.sourceforge.net/*), brings many open source packages to Mac OS X.) You can thus do much more at a much lower cost.

- Not only are the applications often free, but some Unix (and Unix-compatible) operating systems are also free. Linux and FreeBSD are good examples. Like the free applications, most free Unix versions are of excellent quality. They're maintained by volunteer programmers and corporations who want a powerful OS and are frustrated by the slow, bug-ridden OS development at some big software companies. Mac OS X's Darwin core qualifies as a free Unix (you can get it at *http://developer.apple.com/darwin/*), but it does not have Mac OS X's easy-to-use interface. Many people use Mac OS X daily without ever knowing about all the power lurking under the hood.

- Unix runs on almost any kind of computer, from tiny embedded systems to giant supercomputers. After you read this book, you'll not only know all about Darwin, but you'll also be ready to use many other kinds of Unix-based computers without learning a new OS for each one.

- In general, Unix (especially without a windowing system) is less resource intensive than other major operating systems. For instance, Linux will run happily on an old system with an Intel 80386 microprocessor and let multiple users share the same computer. (Don't bother trying to use the latest versions of Microsoft Windows on a system that's more than a few years old!) If you need a windowing system, Unix lets you choose from modern feature-rich interfaces as well as from simple ones that need much less system power. Anyone with limited resources—educational institutions, organizations in developing countries, and so on—can use Unix to do more with less.

- Much of the Internet's development was done on Unix systems. Many Internet web sites and Internet service providers use Unix because it's so flexible and inexpensive. With powerful hardware, Unix really shines.

Versions of Unix

There are several versions of Unix. Some past and present commercial versions include Solaris, AIX, and HP/UX. Freely available versions include Linux, NetBSD, OpenBSD, and FreeBSD. Darwin, the free Unix underneath Mac OS X, was built by grafting an advanced version called Mach onto BSD, with a light sprinkling of Apple magic for the windowing system.

Although graphical user interfaces (GUIs) and advanced features differ among Unix systems, you should be able to use much of what you learn from this introductory handbook on any system. Don't worry too much about what's from what version of Unix. Just as English borrows words from French, German, Japanese, Italian, and even Hebrew, Mac OS X Unix borrows commands from many different versions of Unix, but you can just use them all without paying attention to their origins.

We do from time to time explain features of Unix on other systems. Knowing the differences can help you if you ever want to use another type of Unix system. When we write "Unix" in this book, we mean "Unix and its versions" unless we specifically mention a particular version.

Interfaces to Unix

Unix can be used as it was originally designed: on typewriter-like terminals, from a prompt on a command line. Most versions of Unix also work with window systems (or GUIs). These allow each user to have a single screen with multiple windows—including "terminal" windows that act like the original Unix interface.

Mac OS X includes a simple terminal application for accessing the command-line level of the system. That application, reasonably enough, is called Terminal and can be found in the Applications → Utilities folder. The Terminal application will be examined more closely in Chapters 1 and 2.

Although you can certainly use your Mac quite efficiently without typing text at a shell prompt, we'll spend all our time in this book on that traditional command-line interface to Unix. Why?

- Every Unix system has a command-line interface. If you know how to use the command line, you'll always be able to use the system.
- If you become a more advanced Unix user, you'll find that the command line is actually much more flexible than a windowing interface. Unix programs are designed to be used together from the command line—as "building blocks"—in an almost infinite number of combinations, to do an infinite number of tasks. No windowing system we've seen (yet!) has this tremendous power.
- You can launch and close GUI programs from the command line.
- Once you learn to use the command line, you can use those same techniques to write *scripts*. These little (or big!) programs automate jobs you'd have to do manually and repetitively with a window system (unless you understand how to program a window system, which is usually a much harder job). See the section "Programming" in Chapter 10 for a brief introduction to scripting.
- In general, text-based interfaces are much easier than GUIs for sight-impaired users.

We aren't saying that the command-line interface is right for every situation. For instance, using the Web—with its graphics and links—is usually easier with a GUI web browser within Mac OS X. But the command line is the fundamental way to use Unix. Understanding it will let you work on any Unix system, with or without windows. A great resource for general Mac OS X information (the GUI you're probably used to) can be found in *Mac OS X: The Missing Manual* by David Pogue (Pogue Press/O'Reilly).

What This Handbook Covers

This book teaches basic system utility commands to get you started with Unix, specifically Darwin. Instead of overwhelming you with lots of details, we want you to be comfortable in the Unix environment as soon as possible.

So we cover a command's most useful features instead of describing all its options in detail.

We also assume that your computer works properly; you have started it, know the procedure for turning the power off, and know how to perform system maintenance. In other words, we don't cover Unix system administration or Mac system administration from the command line.

Without making substantial changes to Mac OS X, Darwin users are constrained to using Aqua (the standard Mac system) as the graphical interface to the system. On a non-Mac Unix system, users can choose between many different user interfaces—shells and window systems. If you do advanced work or set up Unix systems for other users, we recommend learning about a variety of shells and window systems and choosing the best ones for your needs. The principles explained in this book should help you use any Unix configuration.

Format

The following sections describe conventions used in this handbook.

Graphical User Interface Features

While this book spends most of its time on the Unix command line, we do sometimes need to tell you how to run programs from the GUI. We may do this with a compact syntax such as:

> Finder → Applications → Utilities → Terminal

This shorthand should be read as: open the Finder, then choose Applications, then Utilities, then Terminal. We use the same syntax whether the user interface feature to be selected is a window, a menu item, or an icon. The meaning should be obvious from the context. If you don't see a window or icon with the name we give, look at the menu bar. (For example, Terminal → Preferences means to select the Preferences item from the Terminal's menu bar.)

Unix Commands

We introduce each main concept first, then break it down into task-oriented sections. Each section shows the best command to use for a task, explains what it does, and shows the syntax (how to put the command line together). The syntax is given like this:

> rm *filename*

Commands appear in constant width type (in this example, rm). You should type the command exactly as it appears in the example. The variable parts (here, *filename*) will appear in *constant width italic* type; you must supply your own value. To enter this command, you would type rm followed by a space and the name of the file that you want to remove, then press the Return key. (Your keyboard may have a key labeled Enter or an arrow with a right-angle shaft instead of a Return key.) Words in *regular italic* are new terms. Finally, keyboard combinations are indicated with a hyphen; for example, "Control-X" means to hold down the Control key and the X key at the same time. The letter appears capitalized in the book, but you do not have to capitalize it as you type.

Examples

Examples show what should happen as you enter a command. Some examples assume that you've created certain files. If you haven't, you may not get the results shown.

We use typewriter-style characters for examples. In code samples, items you type to try the example are **boldface**. System messages and responses are constant width.

Here's an example:

```
% date
Mon Feb  4 16:17:25 PST 2002
%
```

The character % is the shell (system) prompt. To do this example, you would type date and then press Return. The date command responds "Mon Feb 4 16:17:25 PST 2002" and then returns you to the prompt.

Text you see in examples may not be exactly what you see on your screen. Sometimes we edit screen samples to eliminate distracting text or make them fit the page.

Problem Checklist

We've included problem checklists in some sections. You may skip these parts and go back to them if you have a problem.

Exercises

Some sections have exercises to reinforce the text you've read. Follow the exercises, but don't be afraid to experiment on your own.

Exercises have two columns. The lefthand column tells you what to do and the right-hand column tells you how to do it. For example, a line in the section "Exercise: Entering a Few Commands" near the end of Chapter 1 shows the following:

Get today's date.   date

To follow the exercise, type the word date on your keyboard and press the Return key. The lefthand column tells you what will happen.

After you try the commands, you'll have a better idea of the ones you want to learn more about. You can then get more information from the section "Documentation" in Chapter 10.

Comments and Questions

Please address any comments and questions concerning this book to the publisher:

O'Reilly & Associates, Inc.
1005 Gravenstein Highway North
Sebastopol, CA 95472
(800) 998-9938 (in the United States or Canada)
(707) 829-0515 (international or local)
(707) 829-0104 (fax)

To ask technical questions or comment on the book, send email to:

bookquestions@oreilly.com

We have a web site for the book where examples, errata, and any plans for future editions are listed. You can access this site at:

http://www.oreilly.com/catalog/lunixmacosx2/

For more information about books, conferences, Resource Centers, and the O'Reilly Network, see the O'Reilly web site at:

http://www.oreilly.com

If you write to us, please include information about your Unix environment and the computer you use. You'll have our thanks, along with thanks from future readers of this handbook.

The Evolution of This Book

This book is based on the popular O'Reilly title *Learning the Unix Operating System*, by Jerry Peek, Grace Todino, and John Strang (currently in its fifth edition). There are many differences in this book to meet the needs of Mac OS X users, but the fundamental layout and explanations are the same.

Acknowledgments for Dave Taylor

I'd like to acknowledge the great work of Laurie Petrycki, the editor at O'Reilly, and the valuable information and review of the manuscript by Apple Computer, Inc. In addition, Justin Walker, Eugene Lee, David Mackler, and Adriaan Tijsseling offered helpful insight on the printer and sendmail configuration puzzles. I would also like to express my gratitude to Chuck Toporek and Chris Stone for their valuable comments on the draft manuscript. Thanks also to Christian Crumlish for his back-room assistance, and Tim O'Reilly for the opportunity to help revise the popular *Learning the Unix Operating System* book for the exciting new Mac OS X world. Oh, and a big grin to Linda, Ashley, and Gareth for letting me type, type, and type some more, ultimately getting this book out the door in a remarkably speedy manner.

Acknowledgments for Brian Jepson

I'd like to thank Nathan Torkington, my editor, for helping me shape, launch, and complete this project. Also, thanks to Laurie Petrycki and John Osborn for helping me shuffle around my other projects to make the time to work on this. Thanks to Chris Stone, Chuck Toporek, and employees of Apple Computer, Inc., for their valuable feedback on this book. My appreciation goes out to Jane Ellin who made sure we had a smooth ride between the time I closed the last chapter in FrameMaker and the time the book went off to the printer. Special thanks to Joan, Seiji, and Yeuhi for letting me slip away into various corners of the house as I worked on this book.

## CHAPTER 1

Getting Started

With a typical Unix system, a staff person has to set up a Unix *account* for you before you can use it. With Mac OS X, however, the operating system installation automatically creates a default user account. The account is identified by your *username*, which is usually a single word or an abbreviation. Think of this account as your office—it's your personal place in the Unix environment.

When you log in to your Mac OS X system, you're automatically logged into your Unix account as well. In fact, your Desktop and other customized features of your Mac OS X environment have corresponding features in the Unix environment. Your files and programs can be accessed either through the Mac Finder or through a variety of Unix command-line utilities that you can reach from within Mac OS X's Terminal window.

Working in the Unix Environment

To get into the Unix environment, launch the Terminal application. (That's Finder → Applications → Utilities → Terminal. If you expect to use the Terminal a lot, drag the Terminal icon from the Finder window onto the Dock. You can then launch Terminal with a single click.) Once Terminal is running, you'll see a window like the one in Figure 1-1.

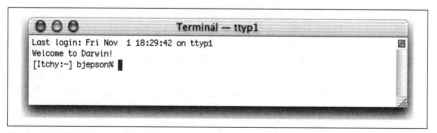

Figure 1-1. The Terminal window

Once you have a window open and you're typing commands, it's helpful to know that regular Mac OS X copy and paste commands work, so it's simple to send an email message to a colleague showing your latest Unix interaction, or to paste some text from a web page into a file you're editing with a Unix text editor such as vi.

You can also have a number of different Terminal windows open if that helps your workflow. Simply use ⌘-N to open each one, and ⌘-~ to cycle between them without removing your hands from the keyboard.

If you have material in your scroll buffer you want to find, use ⌘-F (or select Find → Find from the Edit menu) and enter the specific text. ⌘-G (Find Next) lets you search down the scroll buffer for the next occurrence, and ⌘-D (Find Previous) lets you search up the scroll buffer for the previous occurrence. You can also search for material by highlighting a passage, entering ⌘-E (Use Selection for Find) or jumping to the selected material with ⌘-J (Jump to Selection). You can also save an entire Terminal session as a text file with File → Save Text As, and you can print the entire session with File → Print. It's a good idea to study the key sequences shown in the Scrollback menu, as illustrated in Figure 1-2.

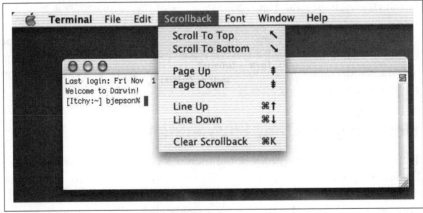

Figure 1-2. Command sequences accessible from the Scrollback menu

Inside the Terminal window, you're working with a program called a *shell*. The shell interprets command lines you enter, runs programs you ask for, and generally coordinates what happens between you and the Unix operating system. The default shell on Mac OS X is called *tcsh* (this could change in future versions of Mac OS X). Other available shells include the Bourne shell (*sh*), the C shell (*csh*), the Bourne-Again shell (*bash*), and the Z Shell (*zsh*). A popular shell on other versions of Unix (not available by default on

Mac OS X) is the Korn shell (*ksh*). To change the shell that Terminal uses, see "Launching Terminal" in Chapter 4.

For a beginner, differences between shells are slight. If you plan to work with Unix a lot, though, you should learn more about your shell and its special commands.

 To find out which shell you're using, run the command echo $SHELL or ps $$. (See the section "Entering a Command Line," later in this chapter.) The answer, which could be something like */bin/tcsh*, is your shell's name or pathname.

The Shell Prompt

When the system is ready to run a command, the shell outputs a *prompt* to tell you that you can enter a command.

The default prompt in *tcsh* is the computer name (which might be something automatically generated, such as dhcp-254-108, or a name you've given your system), the current directory (which might be represented by ~, Unix's shorthand for your home directory), your login name, and a percent sign. For example, the complete prompt might look like this: [limbo:~] taylor%. The prompt can be customized, though, so your own shell prompt may be different. We'll show you how to customize your prompt in Chapter 4.

A prompt that ends with a hash mark (#) usually means you're logged in as the *superuser*. The superuser doesn't have the protections for standard users that are built into the Unix system. If you don't know Unix well, you can inadvertently damage your system software when you are logged in as the superuser. In this case, we recommend that you stop work until you've found out how to access your personal Unix account. The simplest solution is to open a new Terminal window (File → New Shell) and work in that window. If you've still got the superuser prompt, it means that someone either logged into Mac OS X as the superuser or your shell prompt has been customized to end with a # even when you're not the superuser. Try logging out of Mac OS X (→ Log Out) and logging back in.

Entering a Command Line

Entering a command line at the shell prompt tells the computer what to do. Each command line includes the name of a Unix program. When you press Return, the shell interprets your command line and executes the program.

The first word that you type at a shell prompt is always a Unix command (or program name). Like most things in Unix, program names are case sensitive; if the program name is lowercase (and most are), you must type it in lowercase. Some simple command lines have just one word, which is the program name. For more information, see the section "Syntax of Unix Command Lines," later in this chapter.

date

An example single-word command is date. Entering the command date displays the current date and time:

```
% date
Fri Nov  1 16:26:55 EST 2002
%
```

As you type a command line, the system simply collects your keyboard input. Pressing the Return key tells the shell that you've finished entering text, and it can run the program.

who

Another simple command is who. It displays a list of each logged-on user's username, terminal number, and login time. Try it now, if you'd like.

The who program can also tell you which account is currently using the Terminal application, in case you have multiple user accounts on your Mac. The command line for this is who am i. This command line consists of the command (who, the program's name) and arguments (am i). (Arguments are explained in the section "Syntax of Unix Command Lines" later in this chapter.) For example:

```
% who am i
taylor    ttyp1    Nov  1 16:26
```

The response shown in this example says that:

- "I am" Taylor (actually, my username is *taylor*). The username is the same as the Short Name you're asked to define when you create a new user with System Preferences → Accounts → New User.
- I'm using terminal p1. (This cryptic syntax, ttyp1, is a holdover from the early days of Unix. All you need to know as a Unix beginner is that each time you open a new terminal window, the number at the end of the name gets incremented. The first one by ttyp1, the second ttyp2, and so on. The terminal ID also appears in the titlebar of the Terminal window.)
- I opened a new Terminal window at 4:26 in the afternoon of November 1.

Recalling Previous Commands

Modern Unix shells remember command lines you've typed previously. They can even remember commands from previous login sessions. This handy feature can save you a lot of retyping of common commands. As with many things in Unix, though, there are several different ways to do this; we don't have room to show and explain them all. You can get more information from sources listed in Chapter 10.

After you've typed and executed several command lines, try pressing the up-arrow key on your keyboard. You will see the previous command line after your shell prompt, just as you typed it before. Pressing the up-arrow again recalls the previous command line, and so on. Also, as you'd expect, the down-arrow key will recall more recent command lines.

To execute one of these remembered commands, just press the Return key. (Your cursor doesn't have to be at the end of the command line.)

Once you've recalled a command line, you can edit it. If you don't want to execute any remembered commands, cancel the command line with Control-C or ⌘-.. The next section explains both of these.

Correcting a Command Line

What if you make a mistake in a command line? Suppose you typed dare instead of date and pressed the Return key before you realized your mistake. The shell will give you an error message:

```
% dare
dare: command not found
%
```

Don't be too concerned about getting error messages. Sometimes you'll get an error even if it appears that you typed the command correctly. This can be caused by typing control characters that are invisible on the screen. Once the prompt returns, reenter your command.

As we said earlier (in the section "Recalling Previous Commands"), you can recall previous commands and edit command lines. Use the up-arrow to recall a previous command.

To edit the command line, use the left-arrow and right-arrow keys to move your cursor to the point where you want to make a change. You can use the Delete key to erase characters to the left of the cursor.

If you have logged into your Macintosh remotely from another system (see Chapter 7), your keyboard may be different. The erase character differs between systems and accounts, and can be customized. The most common erase characters are:

- Delete or Del
- Control-H

Control-C or ⌘-. will interrupt or cancel a command and can be used in many (but not all) cases when you want to quit what you're doing.

Other common control characters are:

Control-U
> Erases the whole input line; you can start over.

Control-S
> Pauses output from a program that's writing to the screen. This can be confusing; we don't recommend using Control-S, but want you to be aware of it.

Control-Q
> Restarts output after a Control-S pause.

Control-D
> Signals the end of input for some programs (such as cat, explained in the section "Putting Text in a File" in Chapter 6) and returns you to a shell prompt. If you type Control-D at a shell prompt, it may close your current Terminal window.

Ending Your Session

To end a Unix session, you must exit the Terminal. You should *not* end a session by just quitting the Terminal application or closing the terminal window. It's possible that you might have started a process running in the background (see Chapter 9), and closing the window will interrupt the process so it won't complete. Instead, type exit at a shell prompt. The window will either close or display [Process completed]; then you can then safely quit the Terminal application. If you've started a background process, you'll instead get one of the messages in the Problem Checklist below.

Problem checklist

The first few times you use Mac OS X, you aren't likely to have the following problems. But you may encounter these problems later, as you do more advanced work.

You get another shell prompt, or the shell says "logout: not login shell."
> You've been using a subshell (a shell created by your original Terminal shell). To end each subshell, type exit (or just type Control-D) until the Terminal window closes.

The shell says "There are stopped jobs" or "There are running jobs."
Mac OS X and many other Unix systems have a feature called *job control* that lets you suspend a program temporarily while it's running or keep it running separately in the "background." One or more programs you ran during your session has not ended but is stopped (paused) or in the background. Enter fg to bring each stopped job into the foreground, then quit the program normally. (See Chapter 9 for more information.)

The Terminal application refuses to quit, saying "Closing this window will terminate the following processes inside it:", followed by a list of programs.
Terminal tries to help by not quitting when you're in the middle of running a command. Cancel the dialog box and make sure you don't have any commands running that you forgot about.

Syntax of Unix Command Lines

Unix command lines can be simple, one-word entries such as the date command. They can also be more complex; you may need to type more than the command or program name.*

A Unix command can have *arguments*. An argument can be an option or a filename. The general format for a Unix command line is:

```
command option(s) filename(s)
```

There isn't a single set of rules for writing Unix commands and arguments, but these general rules work in most cases:

- Enter commands in lowercase.

- *Options* modify the way in which a command works. Options are often single letters prefixed with a dash (-, also called "hyphen" or "minus") and set off by any number of spaces or tabs. Multiple options in one command line can be set off individually (such as -a -b). In some cases, you can combine them after a single dash (such as -ab), but most commands' documentation doesn't tell you whether this will work; you'll have to try it.

  Some commands also have options made from complete words or phrases and starting with two dashes, such as --delete or --confirm-delete. When you enter a command line, you can use this option style, the single-letter options (which each start with a single dash), or both.

---

* The command can be the name of a Unix program (such as date), or it can be a command that's built into the shell (such as exit). You probably don't need to worry about this! You can read more precise definitions of these terms and others in the Glossary.

- The argument *filename* is the name of a file you want to use. Most Unix programs also accept multiple filenames, separated by spaces or specified with wildcards (see Chapter 3). If you don't enter a filename correctly, you may get a response such as "*filename*: no such file or directory" or "*filename*: cannot open."

  Some commands, such as telnet and who (shown earlier in this chapter), have arguments that aren't filenames.

- You must type spaces between commands, options, and filenames. You'll need to "quote" filenames that contain spaces. For more information, see the section "File and Directory Names" in Chapter 3.

- Options come before filenames.

- In a few cases, an option has another argument associated with it; type this special argument just after its option. Most options don't work this way, but you should know about them. The sort command is an example of this feature: you can tell sort to write the sorted text to a filename given after its -o option. In the following example, sort reads the file *sortme* (given as an argument), and writes to the file *sorted* (given after the -o option):

  ```
  % sort -o sorted -n sortme
  ```

  We also used the -n option in that example. But -n is a more standard option; it has nothing to do with the final argument *sortme* on that command line. So, we also could have written the command line this way:

  ```
  % sort -n -o sorted sortme
  ```

  Don't be too concerned about these special cases, though. If a command needs an option like this, its documentation will say so.

- Command lines can have other special characters, some of which we see later in this book. They can also have several separate commands. For instance, you can write two or more commands on the same command line, each separated by a semicolon (;). Commands entered this way are executed one after another by the shell.

Mac OS X has a lot of commands! Don't try to memorize all of them. In fact, you'll probably need to know just a few commands and their options. As time goes on, you'll learn these commands and the best way to use them for your job. We cover some useful commands in later chapters. This book's quick reference card has quick reminders.

Let's look at a sample command. The ls program displays a list of files. You can use it with or without options and arguments. If you enter:

```
% ls
```

you'll see a list of filenames. But if you enter:

```
% ls -l
```

there'll be an entire line of information for each file. The -l option (a dash and a lowercase letter "L") changes the normal ls output to a long format. You can also get information about a particular file by using its name as the second argument. For example, to find out about a file called *chap1*, enter:

```
% ls -l chap1
```

Many Unix commands have more than one option. For instance, ls has the -a (all) option for listing hidden files. You can use multiple options in either of these ways:

```
% ls -a -l
% ls -al
```

You must type one space between the command name and the dash that introduces the options. If you enter ls-al, the shell will say "ls-al: command not found."

Exercise: Entering a Few Commands

The best way to get used to the Terminal is to enter some commands. To run a command, type the command and then press the Return key. Remember that almost all Unix commands are typed in lowercase.

Here are a few to try:

Task	Command
Get today's date.	date
List logged-in users.	who
Obtain more information about users.	who -u, finger, or w
Find out who is at your terminal.	who am i
Enter two commands in the same line.	who am i;date
Mistype a command.	woh

In this session, you've tried several simple commands and seen the results on the screen.

Types of Commands

When you use a program, you'll want to know how to control it. How can you tell it what job you want done? Do you give instructions before the program starts, or after it's started? There are several general ways to give commands on a Mac OS X system. It's good to be aware of them.

Graphical programs

Some programs work only within the graphical window environment (on Mac OS X, this is called Aqua). On Mac OS X, you can run these programs using the open command. For instance, when you type open -a Chess at a shell prompt, the chess game starts. It opens one or more windows on your screen. The program has its own way to receive your commands—through menus and buttons on its windows, for instance. Although you can't interact with these programs using traditional Unix utilities, Mac OS X includes the osascript utility, which lets you run AppleScript commands from the Unix shell.

Non-interactive Unix programs

You've also seen in the section "Syntax of Unix Command Lines" that you can enter many Unix commands at a shell prompt. These programs work in a window system (from a Terminal window) or from any terminal. You control those programs from the Unix command line—that is, by typing options and arguments from a shell prompt before you start the program. After you start the program, wait for it to finish; you generally don't interact with it.

Interactive Unix programs

Some Unix programs that work in the terminal window have commands of their own. (If you'd like some examples, see Chapters 2 and 3.) These programs may accept options and arguments on their command lines. But, once you start a program, it prints its own prompt and/or menus, and it understands its own commands; it takes instructions from your keyboard that weren't given on its command line.

For instance, if you enter ftp at a shell prompt, you'll see a new prompt from the ftp program. Enter FTP commands to transfer files to and from remote systems. When you enter the special command quit to quit the ftp program, ftp will stop prompting you. Then you'll get another shell prompt, where you can enter other Unix commands.

The Unresponsive Terminal

During your Unix session, your terminal may not respond when you type a command, or the display on your screen may stop at an unusual place. That's called a "hung" or "frozen" terminal or session. Note that most of the techniques in this section apply to a terminal window, but not to non-terminal windows such as a web browser.

A session can hang for several reasons. For instance, your computer can get too busy; the Terminal application has to wait its turn. In that case, your session starts by itself after a few moments. You should *not* try to "un-hang" the session by entering extra commands, because those commands will all take effect after Terminal comes back to life.

 If your display becomes garbled, press Control-L. In the shell, this will clear the screen and display the prompt. In a full-screen program, such as a text editor, it will redraw the screen.

If the system doesn't respond for quite a while (how long that is depends on your individual situation; ask other users about their experiences), the following solutions usually work. Try the following steps in the order shown until the system responds:

Press the Return key once.
> You may have typed text at a prompt (for example, a command line at a shell prompt) but haven't yet pressed Return to say that you're done typing and your text should be interpreted.

Try job control (see Chapter 9); type Control-Z.
> This control key sequence suspends a program that may be running and gives you a shell prompt. Now you can enter the jobs command to find the program's name, then restart the program with fg or terminate it with kill.

Press Control-C or ⌘–..
> This interrupts a program that may be running. (Unless the program is run in the background; as described in the section, "Running a Command in the Background" in Chapter 9, the shell waits for a background program to finish before giving a new prompt. A long-running background program may thus appear to hang the terminal.) If this doesn't work the first time, try it once more; doing it more than twice usually won't help.

Type Control-Q.
> If output has been stopped with Control-S, this will restart it. (Note that some systems will automatically issue Control-S if they need to pause output; this character may not have been typed from the keyboard.)

Type Control-D once at the beginning of a new line.
> Some programs (such as mail) expect text from the user. A program may be waiting for an end-of-input character from you to tell it that you've finished entering text. Typing Control-D may cause you to log out, so you should try this only as a last resort.

Otherwise, close your Terminal window and open a new one.

CHAPTER 2
Using Unix

Once you launch Terminal, you can use the many facilities that Mac OS X provides. As a user, you have an account that gives you:

- A place in the filesystem where you can store your files
- A username that identifies you and lets you control access to your files
- An environment you can customize

The Mac OS X Filesystem

A *file* is the unit of storage in Mac OS X. A file can hold anything: text (a report you're writing, a to-do list), a program, digitally encoded pictures or sound, and so on. All of those are just sequences of raw data until they're interpreted by the right program.

Files are organized into directories (more commonly referred to as a *folder* on the Mac). A *directory* is actually a special kind of file where the system stores information about other files. You can think of a directory as a place, so that files are said to be contained *in* directories, and you work *inside* a directory.

A *filesystem* includes all the files and directories on a mounted volume, such as your system's hard disk or your iDisk. This section introduces the Mac OS X filesystem. Later sections show how you can look in files and protect them. Chapter 3 has more information.

Your Home Directory

When you launch Terminal, you're placed in a directory called your *home directory*. This directory, which can be opened in the Finder by clicking the Home icon, contains personal files, application preferences, and application data such as bookmarks. In your home directory, you can create your own files. As you'll see, you can also create directories within your home directory. Like folders in a file cabinet, this is a good way to organize your files.

Your Working Directory

Your *working directory* (also called your current directory) is the directory in which you're currently working. Every time you open a new Terminal window, your home directory is your working directory. When you change to another directory, the directory you move to becomes your working directory.

Unless you specify otherwise, all commands that you enter apply to the files in your working directory. In the same way, when you create files, they're created in your working directory unless you specify another directory. For instance, if you type the command vi report, the vi editor is started, and a file named *report* is created in your working directory. But if you type a command such as vi /Users/john/Documents/report, a *report* file is created in a different directory—without changing your working directory. You'll learn more about this when we cover pathnames later in this chapter.

If you have more than one Terminal window open, each session has its own working directory. Changing the working directory in one session doesn't affect other Terminal windows.

The Directory Tree

All directories on a Mac OS X system are organized into a hierarchical structure that you can imagine as a family tree. The parent directory of the tree (the directory that contains all other directories) is known as the *root directory* and is written as a forward slash (/). The root directory is what you see if you open a new Finder window, click the Computer icon, and then open your startup disk.

The root directory contains several other directories. Figure 2-1 shows a visual representation of the top of the Mac OS X filesystem tree: the root directory and some directories under the root. (To see how this appears in the Finder, see Figure 2-7.)

Applications, Library, Users, and *System* are some of the *subdirectories* (child directories) of the root directory. There are several other directories that are invisible in the Finder but visible at the shell prompt (you can see them if you use the command ls /). These subdirectories are standard Unix directories and include *bin, dev, etc, sbin, tmp, usr,* and *var;* they contain Unix system files. For instance, *bin* contains many Unix programs.

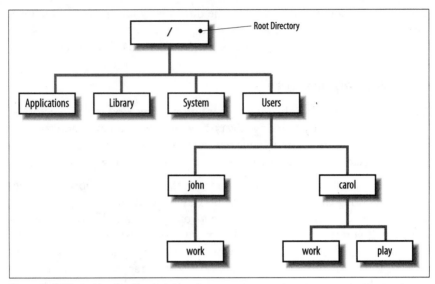

Figure 2-1. Example of a directory tree

In our example, the parent directory of *Users* (one level above) is the root directory. *Users* has two subdirectories (one level below), *john* and *carol*. On a Mac OS X system, each directory has only one parent directory, but it may have one or more subdirectories.*

A subdirectory (such as *carol*) can have its own subdirectories (such as *work* and *play*).

To specify a file or directory location, write its *pathname*. A pathname is like the address of the directory or file in the filesystem. We will look at pathnames in the next section.

On a basic Mac OS X system, all files in the filesystem are stored on disks connected to your computer. Mac OS X has a way to access files on other computers: a *networked filesystem*. Networked filesystems make a remote computer's files appear as if they're part of your computer's directory tree. For instance, when you mount your iDisk (Choose Go → iDisk in the Finder), Mac OS X mounts your iDisk on your desktop, and also makes it available as a directory under */Volumes*. You can also mount shared directories from other Macintoshes or Windows machines (choose Go → Connect to Server in the Finder). These will also appear in the */Volumes* directory, as will other disks, such as external FireWire drives.

---

* The root directory at the top of the tree is *its own* parent.

Absolute Pathnames

As you saw earlier, the Unix filesystem organizes its files and directories in an inverted tree structure with the root directory at the top. An *absolute pathname* tells you the path of directories through which you must travel to get from the root to the directory or file you want. In a pathname, put slashes (/) between the directory names.

For example, */Users/john* is an absolute pathname. It locates one (*only* one!) directory. Here's how:

- The root is the first slash (/).
- The directory *Users* (a subdirectory of *root*) is second.
- The directory *john* (a subdirectory of *Users*) is last.

Be sure that you do not type spaces anywhere in the pathname. If there are spaces in one or more of the directories, you need to either quote the entire directory pathname, or preface each space with a backslash to ensure that the shell understands that the spaces are part of the pathname itself.

Figure 2-2 shows this structure.

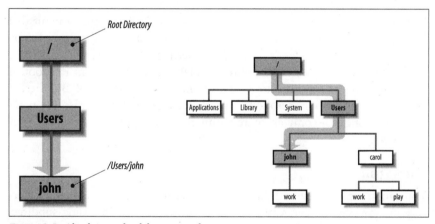

Figure 2-2. Absolute path of directory john

In Figure 2-2, you'll see that the directory *john* has a subdirectory named *work*. Its absolute pathname is */Users/john/work*.

The root is always indicated by the slash (/) at the start of the pathname. In other words, an absolute pathname always starts with a slash.

Relative Pathnames

You can also locate a file or directory with a *relative pathname*. A relative pathname gives the location relative to your working directory.

Unless you use an absolute pathname (starting with a slash), Unix assumes that you're using a relative pathname. Like absolute pathnames, relative pathnames can go through more than one directory level by naming the directories along the path.

For example, if you're currently in the *Users* directory (see Figure 2-2), the relative pathname to the *carol* directory below is simply *carol*. The relative pathname to the *play* directory below that is *carol/play*.

Notice that neither pathname in the previous paragraph starts with a slash. That's what makes them relative pathnames! Relative pathnames start at the working directory, not the root directory. In other words, a relative pathname never starts with a slash.

Pathname puzzle

Here's a short but important question. The previous example explains the relative pathname *carol/play*. What do you think Unix would say about the pathname */carol/play*? (Look again at Figure 2-2.)

Unix would say "No such file or directory." Why? (Please think about that before you read more. It's very important and it's one of the most common beginner's mistakes.) Here's the answer. Because it starts with a slash, the pathname */carol/play* is an absolute pathname that starts from the root. It says to look in the root directory for a subdirectory named *carol*. But there is no subdirectory named *carol* one level directly below the root, so the pathname is wrong. The only absolute pathname to the *play* directory is */Users/carol/play*.

Relative pathnames up

You can go up the tree with the shorthand .. (dot dot) for the parent directory. As you saw earlier, you can also go down the tree by using subdirectory names. In either case (up or down), separate each level by a / (slash).

Figure 2-3 shows part of Figure 2-1. If your working directory in the figure is *work*, then there are two pathnames for the *play* subdirectory of *carol*. You already know how to write the absolute pathname, */Users/carol/play*. You can also go up one level (with ..) to *carol*, then go down the tree to *play*. Figure 2-3 illustrates this.

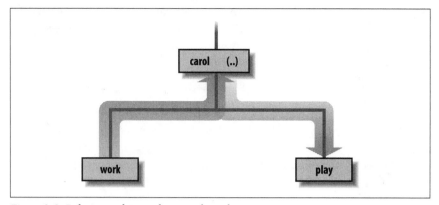

Figure 2-3. Relative pathname from work to play

The relative pathname would be *../play*. It would be wrong to give the relative address as *carol/play*. Using *carol/play* would say that *carol* is a subdirectory of your working directory instead of what it is in this case: the parent directory.

Absolute and relative pathnames are interchangeable. Unix programs simply follow whichever path you specify to wherever it leads. If you use an absolute pathname, the path starts from the root. If you use a relative pathname, the path starts from your current working directory. Choose whichever is easier at the moment.

Changing Your Working Directory

Once you know the absolute or relative pathname of a directory where you'd like to work, you can move up and down the Mac OS X filesystem to reach it. The following sections explain some helpful commands for navigating through a directory tree.

pwd

To find which directory you're currently in, use pwd (print working directory), which prints the absolute pathname of your working directory. The pwd command takes no arguments:

```
% pwd
/Users/john
%
```

cd

You can change your working directory to any directory (including another user's directory, if you have permission) with the cd (change directory) command, which has the form:

```
cd pathname
```

The argument is an absolute or a relative pathname (whichever is easier) for the directory you want to change to:

```
% cd /Users/carol
% pwd
/Users/carol
% cd work
% pwd
/Users/carol/work
%
```

 The command cd, with no arguments, takes you to your home directory from wherever you are in the filesystem.

Note that you can only change to another directory. You cannot cd to a filename. If you try, your shell (in this example, *tcsh*) gives you an error message:

```
% cd /etc/manpath.config
/etc/manpath.config:  Not a directory.
%
```

/etc/manpath.config is a file with information about the configuration of the man command.

One neat trick worth mentioning is that you can always have Terminal enter the path directly by dragging a file or folder icon from the Finder onto the active Terminal window.

Files in the Directory Tree

A directory can hold subdirectories. And, of course, a directory can hold files. Figure 2-4 is a close-up of the filesystem around *john*'s home directory. The four files are shown along with the *work* subdirectory.

Pathnames to files are made the same way as pathnames to directories. As with directories, files' pathnames can be absolute (starting from the root directory) or relative (starting from the working directory). For example, if your working directory is *Users*, the relative pathname to the *work* directory below would be *john/work*. The relative pathname to the *ch1* file would be *john/ch1*.

Unix filesystems can hold things that aren't directories or files, such as symbolic links (similar to aliases), devices (the */dev* directory contains entries for devices attached to the system), and sockets (network communication channels). You may see some of them as you explore the filesystem. We don't cover those advanced topics in this little book.

Two Ways to Explore Your Filesystem

Every file and folder that you view from the Finder is also accessible from the Unix shell. Changes made in one environment are reflected (almost) immediately in the other. For example, the Desktop folder is also the Unix directory */Users/yourname/Desktop*.

Just for fun, open a Finder window, move to your *Desktop* folder, and keep it visible while you type these commands at the shell prompt:

```
% cd
% cd Desktop
% touch mac-rocks
```

Switch back to the Finder (you can click on the desktop) and watch a file called *mac-rocks* appear magically on the Desktop. (The touch command creates an empty file with the name you specify.)

Now type:

```
% rm mac-rocks
```

return to the Finder, and watch the file disappear. The rm command removes the file.

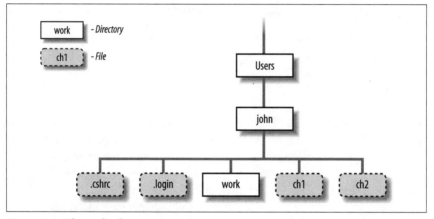

Figure 2-4. Files in the directory tree

Listing Files with ls

To use the cd command, you must know which entries in a directory are subdirectories and which are files. The ls command lists entries in the directory tree and can also show you which is which.

When you enter the ls command, you get a list of the files and subdirectories contained in your working directory. The syntax is:

```
ls option(s) directory-and-filename(s)
```

If you've just moved into an empty directory, entering ls without any arguments may seem to do nothing. This isn't surprising, because you haven't made any files in your working directory. If you have no files, nothing is displayed; you'll simply get a new shell prompt:

```
% ls
%
```

But if you're in your home directory, ls displays the names of the files and directories in that directory. The output depends on what's in your directory. The screen should look something like this:

```
% ls
Desktop    Documents    Library    Movies    Music    Pictures    Public
%
```

Sometimes ls might display filenames in a single column. If yours does, you can make a multicolumn display with the -C (uppercase "C") option or the -x option. ls has a lot of options that change the information and display format.

The -a option (for all) is guaranteed to show you some more files, as in the following example:

```
% ls -a
.                ..           .Trash    .tcsh_history
Desktop          Documents    Library   Movies
Music            Pictures     Public
%
```

When you use ls -a, you'll always see at least two entries with the names . (dot) and .. (dot dot). As mentioned earlier, .. is always the relative pathname to the parent directory. A single . always stands for its working directory; this is useful with commands such as cp (see the section "Copying Files" in Chapter 3). There may also be other files, such as *.tcshrc* or *.Trash*. Any entry whose name begins with a dot is hidden—it's listed only if you use ls -a.

To get more information about each item that ls lists, add the -l option. (That's a lowercase "L" for "long.") This option can be used alone, or in combination with -a, as shown in Figure 2-5. Because *.tcshrc* and *.Trash* are hidden files, only *ch1* and *ch2* would appear if you viewed this directory in the Finder.

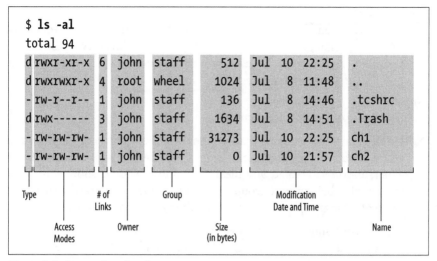

```
$ ls -al
total 94
d rwxr-xr-x  6  john  staff       512  Jul 10  22:25  .
d rwxrwxr-x  4  root  wheel      1024  Jul  8  11:48  ..
- rw-r--r--  1  john  staff       136  Jul  8  14:46  .tcshrc
d rwx------  3  john  staff      1634  Jul  8  14:51  .Trash
- rw-rw-rw-  1  john  staff     31273  Jul 10  22:25  ch1
- rw-rw-rw-  1  john  staff         0  Jul 10  21:57  ch2
```

Type   # of   Group   Modification   Name
              Links   Date and Time

        Access   Owner   Size
        Modes   (in bytes)

Figure 2-5. Output from ls -al

The long format provides the following information about each item:

Total n
> *n* is the amount of storage used by everything in this directory. (This is measured in *blocks*.) On Mac OS X, blocks are 1,024 bytes in size.

Type
> Tells whether the item is a directory (d) or a plain file (-). (There are other less common types that we don't explain here.)

Access modes
> Specifies three types of users (yourself, your group, all others) who are allowed to read (r), write (w), or execute (x) your files or directories. We'll talk more about access modes later.

Links
> The number of files or directories linked to this one. (This isn't the same as a web page link. We don't discuss filesystem links in this little book.)

Owner
> The user who created or owns this file or directory.

Group
> The group that owns the file or directory.

Size (in bytes)
> The size of the file or directory. (A directory is actually a special type of file. Here, the "size" of a directory is of the directory file itself, not the total of all the files in that directory.)

Modification date
> The date when the file was last modified, or when the directory contents last changed (when something in the directory was added, renamed, or removed). If an entry was modified more than six months ago, ls shows the year instead of the time.

Name
> The name of the file or directory.

Notice especially the columns that list the owner and group of the files, and the access modes (also called permissions). The person who creates a file is its owner; if you've created any files, this column should show your username. You also belong to a group. Files you create are marked either with the name of your group or, in some cases, the group that owns the directory.

The permissions show who can read, write, or execute the file or directory. The permissions have 10 characters. The first character shows the file type (d for directory or - for a plain file). The other characters come in groups of three. The first group, characters 2–4, shows the permissions for the file's owner, which is you if you created the file. The second group, characters 5–7, shows permissions for other members of the file's group. The third group, characters 8–10, shows permissions for all other users.

For example, the permissions for *.tcshrc* in Figure 2-5 are -rw-r--r--. The first hyphen, -, indicates that it's a plain file. The next three characters, rw-, mean that the owner, *john*, has both read (r) and write (w) permissions. The next two sets of permissions are both r--, which means that other users who belong to the file's group *staff*, as well as all other users of the system, can only read the file; they don't have write permission, so they can't change what's in the file. No one has execute (x) permission, which should be used only for executable files (programs) and directories.

In the case of directories, x means the permission to access the directory—for example, to run a command that reads a file there or to use a subdirectory. Notice that the first directory shown in Figure 2-5 is executable (accessible) by *john*, by users in the *staff* group, and by everyone else on the system. A directory with write (w) permission allows deleting, renaming, or adding files within the directory. Read (r) permission allows listing the directory with ls.

You can use the chmod command to change the permissions of your files and directories. (See the section "Protecting and Sharing Files" later in this chapter.)

If you need to know only which files are directories and which are executable files, you can use the -F option with ls. If you give the pathname to a directory, ls lists the directory but does *not* change your working directory. The pwd command here shows this:

```
% ls -F /Users/andy
calendar    goals    ideas/
ch2         guide/   testpgm*
% pwd
/Applications
%
```

ls -F puts a / (slash) at the end of each directory name. (The directory name doesn't really have a slash in it; that's just the shorthand ls -F uses to identify a directory.) In our example, *guide* and *ideas* are directories. You can verify this by using ls -l and noting the d in the first field of the output. Files with an execute status (x), such as programs, are marked with an * (asterisk). The file *testpgm* is an executable file. Files that aren't marked are not executable.

ls -R (recursive) lists a directory and all its subdirectories. This can make a very long list—especially when you list a directory near the root! (Piping the output of ls to a pager program solves this problem. There's an example in the section "Piping to a Pager" in Chapter 6.) You can combine other options with -R; for instance, ls -RF marks each directory and file type, while recursively listing files and directories.

Calculating File Size

You can find the size of a file with the du command:

```
% du Documents/Outline.doc
300     Documents/Outline.doc
```

The size is reported in kilobytes, so *Outline.doc* is 300k in size. If you give du the name of a directory, it will calculate the sizes of everything in it:

```
% du Library
0    Library/Application Support/AddressBook/Images/CachedMacDotComPhotos
4    Library/Application Support/AddressBook/Images
228  Library/Application Support/AddressBook
...
```

If you want the total for the directory, use -s (summarize):

```
% du -s Library
164892  Library
```

If you'd like separate totals for all directories and files, including hidden ones, use a wildcard pattern that ignores the . (current) and .. (parent) directories (see "Relative pathnames up," earlier in this chapter):

```
% du -s * .[^.]*
0       Applications
1048    Desktop
```

```
18964   Documents
164892  Library
...
12700   .Trash
4       .tcshrc
```

You can also calculate your system's free disk space with df -h (the -h produces more user-friendly output):

```
% df -h
Filesystem           Size  Used Avail Use% Mounted on
/dev/disk1s9         18G   15G  3.9G  79% /
devfs                1.0k  1.0k    0 100% /dev
fdesc                1.0k  1.0k    0 100% /dev
<volfs>              512k  512k    0 100% /.vol
/dev/disk1s10        449M  406M  43M  91% /Volumes/Mac OS 9
```

The first column (Filesystem) shows the Unix device name for the volume. The second column (Size) shows the total disk size, and it's followed by the amount of disk space used up (Used) and the amount that's available (Avail). After that, the Use% column shows the percentage of disk space used, followed by where the volume is mounted (Mounted on).

/ is the root of your filesystem (a volume that is named Macintosh HD by default). /dev contains files that correspond to hardware devices, and /.vol exposes some internals of the Mac OS X filesystem called *HFS+ file ids*. The last entry is a volume called Mac OS 9.

Completing File and Directory Names

Most Unix shells can complete a partly typed file or directory name for you. Different shells have different methods. If you're using the default shell in Mac OS X, *tcsh*, just type the first few letters of the name, then press Tab. If the shell can find just one way to finish the name, it will; your cursor will move to the end of the new name, where you can type more or press Return to run the command. (You can also edit or erase the completed name.)

What happens if more than one file or directory name matches what you've typed so far? The shell will beep at you to tell you that it couldn't find a match. To get a list of all possible completions, try pressing Control-D and you may see a list of all names starting with the characters you've typed so far (you won't see anything if there are no matches). Here's an example from the *tcsh* shell:

```
% ma<Control-D>
mach_init        mailstat         make_smbcodepage makemap
machine          mailstats        make_unicodemap  malloc_history
mail             make             makedbm          man
mailq            make_printerdef  makeinfo         manpath
% ma
```

At this point, you could type another character or two—an i, for example—and then press Control-D once more to list only the mail-related commands.

Exercise: Exploring the Filesystem

You're now equipped to explore the filesystem with cd, ls, and pwd. Take a tour of the directory system, hopping one or many levels at a time, with a mixture of cd and pwd commands.

Task	Command
Go to your home directory.	cd
Find your working directory.	pwd
Change to new working directory with its absolute pathname.	cd /bin
List files in new working directory.	ls
Change directory to root and list it in one step. (Use the command separator: a semicolon.)	cd /; ls
Find your working directory.	pwd
Change to a subdirectory; use its relative pathname.	cd usr
Find your working directory.	pwd
Change to a subdirectory.	cd lib
Find your working directory.	pwd
Give a wrong pathname.	cd xqk
List files in another directory.	ls /bin
Find your working directory (notice that ls didn't change it).	pwd
Return to your home directory.	cd

Looking Inside Files with less

By now, you're probably tired of looking at files from the outside. It's akin to visiting a bookstore and looking at the covers, but never getting to read a word. Let's look at a program for reading text files.

If you want to "read" a long plain text file on the screen, you can use the less command to display one "page" (a Terminal window filled from top to bottom) of text at a time.

If you don't like less, you can try a very similar program named more. In fact, the name less is a play on the name of more, which came first (but less has more features than more). The syntax for less is:

```
less option(s) file(s)
```

less lets you move forward or backward in the files by any number of pages or lines; you can also move back and forth between two or more files specified on the command line. When you invoke less, the first "page" of the file appears. A prompt appears at the bottom of the Terminal window, as in the following example:

```
% less ch03
A file is the unit of storage in Unix, as in most other systems.
A file can hold anything: text (a report you're writing,
  .
  .
  .
  :
```

The basic less prompt is a colon (:); although, for the first screenful, less displays the file's name as a prompt. The cursor sits to the right of this prompt as a signal for you to enter a less command to tell less what to do. To quit, type q.

Like almost everything about less, the prompt can be customized. For example, using the -M starting flag on the less command line makes the prompt show the filename and your position in the file (as a percentage).

If you want this to happen every time you use less, you can set the LESS environment variable to M (without a dash) in your shell setup file. See the section "Customizing Your Shell Environment" in Chapter 4.

You can set or unset most options temporarily from the less prompt. For instance, if you have the short less prompt (a colon), you can enter -M while less is running. less responds "Long prompt (press Return)," and for the rest of the session, less prompts with the filename, line number, and percentage of the file viewed.

To display the less commands and options available on your system, press h (for "help") while less is running. Table 2-1 lists some simple (but still quite useful) commands.

Table 2-1. Useful less commands

Command	Description	Command	Description
SPACE	Display next page	v	Starts the vi editor
Return	Display next line	Control-L	Redisplay current page
nf	Move forward n lines	h	Help
b	Move backward one page	:n	Go to next file on command line
nb	Move backward n lines	:p	Go back to previous file on command line
/word	Search forward for word		
?word	Search backward for word	q	Quit less

Protecting and Sharing Files

Mac OS X makes it easy for users on the same system to share files and directories. For instance, everyone in a group can read documents stored in one of their manager's directories without needing to make their own copies, if the manager has allowed access. There might be no need to fill peoples' email inboxes with file attachments if everyone can access those files directly through the Unix filesystem.

Here's a brief introduction to file security and sharing. If you have critical security needs, or you just want more information, talk to your system staff or see an up-to-date book on Unix security such as *Practical Unix and Internet Security* (O'Reilly).

 Note that any Admin user can use the *sudo* command (see "Superuser Privileges with sudo," later in this chapter) to do anything to any file at any time, no matter what its permissions are. So, access permissions won't keep your private information safe from *everyone*—although let's hope that you can trust the other folks who share your Macintosh!

Directory Access Permissions

A directory's access permissions help to control access to the files and subdirectories in that directory:

- If a directory has read permission, a user can run ls to see what's in the directory and use wildcards to match files in it.

- A directory that has write permission allows users to add, rename, and delete files in the directory.

- To access a directory (that is, to read or write the files in the directory or to run the files if they're programs) a user needs execute permission on that directory. Note that to access a directory, a user must *also* have execute permission to all its parent directories, all the way up to the root.

 Mac OS X includes a shared directory for all users: */Users/ Shared.* You can create files in this directory and modify files you have put there. However, you cannot modify a file there that's owned by another user.

File Access Permissions

The access permissions on a file control what can be done to the file's *contents*. The access permissions on the directory where the file is kept control whether the file can be renamed or removed. (If this seems confusing, think of it this way: the directory is actually a list of files. Adding, renaming, or removing a file changes the contents of the directory. If the directory isn't writable, you can't change that list.)

Read permission controls whether you can read a file's contents. Write permission lets you change a file's contents. A file shouldn't have execute permission unless it's a program or a script.

Setting Permissions with chmod

Once you know what permissions a file or directory needs—and if you're the owner (listed in the third column of ls -l output)—you can change the permissions with the chmod program. If you select a file or directory in the Finder, and then choose File → Get Info (⌘-I), you can also change the permissions using the Ownership & Permissions section of the Get Info dialog (see Figure 2-6).

There are two ways to change permissions: by specifying the permissions to add or delete, or by specifying the exact permissions. For instance, if a directory's permissions are almost correct, but you also need to make it writable by its group, tell chmod to add group-write permission. But if you need to make more than one change to the permissions—for instance, if you want to add read and execute permission but delete write permission—it's easier to set all permissions explicitly instead of changing them one-by-one. The syntax is:

```
chmod permissions file(s)
```

Let's start with the rules; we see examples next. The *permissions* argument has three parts, which you must give in order with no space between.

1. The category of permission you want to change. There are three: the owner's permission (which chmod calls "user," abbreviated u), the group's permission (g), or others' permission (o). To change more than one category, string the letters together, such as go for "group and others," or simply use a to mean "all" (same as ugo).

2. Whether you want to add (+) the permission, delete (-) it, or specify it exactly (=).

3. What permissions you want to affect: read (r), write (w), or execute (x). To change more than one permission, string the letters together—for example, rw for "read and write."

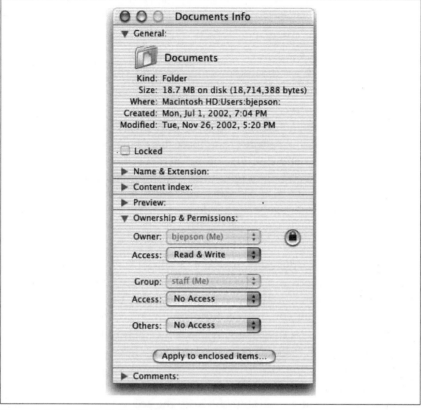

Figure 2-6. The Finder's Get Info dialog

Some examples should make this clearer! In the following command lines, you can replace *dirname* or `filename` with the pathname (absolute or relative) of the directory or file. An easy way to change permissions on the working directory is by using its relative pathname, . (dot), as in chmod o-w .. You can combine two permission changes in the same chmod command by separating them with a comma (,), as shown in the final example.

- To protect a file from accidental editing, delete everyone's write permission with the command:

      chmod a-w *filename*

  On the other hand, if you own an unwritable file that you want to edit, but you don't want to change other peoples' write permissions, you can add "user" (owner) write permission with:

      chmod u+w *filename*

- To keep yourself from accidentally removing files (or adding or renaming files) in an important directory of yours, delete your own write permission with the command:

  ```
  chmod u-w dirname
  ```

  If other users have that permission too, you could delete everyone's write permission with:

  ```
  chmod a-w dirname
  ```

- If you want you and your group to be able to read and write all the files in your working directory—but those files have various permissions now, so adding and deleting the permissions individually would be a pain—this is a good place to use the = operator to set the exact permissions you want. Use the filename wildcard *, which means "everything in this directory" (explained in the section "File and Directory Wildcards" in Chapter 3) and type:

  ```
  chmod ug=rw *
  ```

- If your working directory had any subdirectories, though, that command would be wrong because it takes away execute permission from the subdirectories, so the subdirectories couldn't be accessed anymore. In that case, you could try a more specific wildcard. Or, instead of a wildcard, you can simply list the filenames you want to change, separated by spaces, as in:

  ```
  chmod ug=rw afile bfile cfile
  ```

- To protect the files in a directory and all its subdirectories from everyone else on your system, but still keep the access permissions *you* have there, you could use:

  ```
  chmod go-rwx dirname
  ```

  to delete all "group" and "others" permission to read, write, and execute. A simpler way is to use the command

  ```
  chmod go= dirname
  ```

  to set "group" and "others" permission to exactly nothing.

- You want full access to a directory. Other people on the system should be able to see what's in the directory (and read or edit the files if the file permissions allow it) but not rename, remove, or add files. To do that, give yourself all permissions, but give "group" and "others" only read and execute permission. Use the command:

  ```
  chmod u=rwx,go=rx dirname
  ```

After you change permissions, it's a good idea to check your work with ls -l *filename* or ls -ld *dirname* (without the -d option, ls will list the contents of the directory instead of its permissions and other information).

Problem checklist

I get the message "chmod: Not owner."

> Only the owner of a file or directory (or the superuser) can set its permissions. Use ls -1 to find the owner or use superuser privileges (see "Superuser Privileges with sudo," later in this chapter).

A file is writable, but my program says it can't be written.

> First, check the file permissions with ls -1 and be sure you're in the category (user, group, or others) that has write permission.
>
> The problem may also be in the permissions of the file's directory. Some programs need permission to write more files into the same directory (for example, temporary files), or to rename files (for instance, making a file into a backup) while editing. If it's safe to add write permission to the directory (if other files in the directory don't need protection from removal or renaming) try that. Otherwise, copy the file to a writable directory (with cp), edit it there, then copy it back to the original directory.

Changing Group and Owner

Group ownership lets a certain group of users have access to a file or directory. You might need to let a different group have access. The chgrp program sets the group owner of a file or directory. You can set the group to any of the groups to which you belong. Because you're likely going to be administering your system, you can control the list of groups you're in. (In some situations, the system administrator controls the list of groups you're in.) The groups program lists your groups.

For example, if you're a designer creating a directory named *images* for several illustrators, the directory's original group owner might be *admin*. You'd like the illustrators, all of whom are in the group named *staff*, to access the directory; members of other groups should have no access. Use commands such as:

```
% groups
admin staff
% mkdir images
% ls -ld images
drwxr-xr-x    2 roberts   admin         68 Nov  6 09:53 images
% chgrp staff images
% chmod o= images
% ls -ld images
drwxr-x---    2 roberts   staff         68 Nov  6 09:53 images
```

Many Unix systems also let you set a directory's group ownership so that any files you later create in that directory will be owned by the same group as the directory. Try the command chmod g+s *dirname*. The permissions listing from ls -ld will now show an *s* in place of the second x, such as drwxr-s---.

The chown program changes the owner of a file or directory. Only the superuser can use chown (see "Superuser Privileges with sudo," later in this chapter).[*]

```
% chown eric images
chown: changing ownership of `images': Operation not permitted
% sudo chown eric images
Password:
%
```

Changing Your Password

The ownership and permissions system described in this chapter depends on the security of your username and password. If others get your username and password, they can log into your account and do anything you can. They can read private information, corrupt or delete important files, send email messages as if they came from you, and more. If your computer is connected to a network, whether it be the Internet or a local network inside your organization, intruders may also be able to log in without sitting at your keyboard! See the section "Remote Logins" in Chapter 7 for one way this can be done.

Anyone may be able to get your username—it's usually part of your email address, for instance, or shows up as a file's owner in a long directory listing. Your password is what keeps others from logging in as you. Don't leave your password anywhere around your computer. Don't give your password to anyone who asks you for it unless you're sure he'll preserve your account security. Also don't send your password by email; it can be stored, unprotected, on other systems and on backup tapes, where other people may find it and then break into your account.

If you think that someone knows your password, you should probably change it right away—although if you suspect that a computer "cracker" (or "hacker") is using your account to break into your system, you should ask your system administrator for advice first, if possible. You should also change your password periodically. Every few months is recommended.

---

[*] If you have permission to read another user's file, you can make a copy of it (with cp; see the section "Copying Files" in Chapter 3). You'll own the copy.

A password should be easy for you to remember but hard for other people (or password-guessing programs) to guess. Here are some guidelines. A password should be between six and eight characters long. It should not be a word in any language, a proper name, your phone number, your address, or anything anyone else might know or guess that you'd use as a password. It's best to mix upper- and lowercase letters, punctuation, and numbers. A good way to come up with a unique but memorable password is to think of a phrase that only you might know, and use the first letters of each word (and punctuation) to create the password. For example, consider the password mlwsiF! ("My laptop was stolen in Florence!").

To change your password, you can use System Preferences → Accounts, but you can also change it from the command line using the passwd command. After you enter the command, it prompts you to enter your old password. If the password is correct, it asks you to enter the new password—twice, to be sure there is no typing mistake. For security, neither the old nor the new passwords appear as you type them.

Superuser Privileges with sudo

Your Mac OS X user account runs with restricted privileges; there are parts of the filesystem you don't have access to, and there are certain activities that are prohibited until you supply a password. For example, when you run the Software Update utility from System Preferences, Mac OS X may ask you for your password before it proceeds. This extra authentication step allows Software Update to run installers with superuser privileges.

You can invoke these same privileges at the command line by prefixing a command with sudo, a utility that prompts you for your password and executes the command as the superuser. You must be an Admin user to use sudo. The user you created when you first set up your Mac will be an Admin user. You can add new Admin users, or grant Admin status to a user in System Preferences → Accounts.

 What if you don't know your administrative password? If you forgot your password, read the Mac OS Help to direct you. You might need to reboot your computer off your original Mac OS X install CD-ROM, then when you get to the installer, select the Reset Password... option from the Installer menu. The program will then prompt you for a new password and set it for your machine. Reboot again (without the CD-ROM), and you should be set forever.

You may need to use sudo when you install Unix utilities or if you want to modify a file you don't own. Suppose that you accidentally created a file in the */Users* directory while you were doing something else as the superuser. You won't be able to modify it with your normal privileges, so you'll need to use sudo:

```
% ls -l logfile.out
-rw-r--r--   1 root      wheel      1784064 Nov  6 11:25 logfile.out
% rm logfile.out
override rw-r--r--  root/wheel for logfile.out? y
rm: logfile.out: Permission denied
% sudo rm logfile.out
Password:********
% ls -l logfile.out
ls: logfile.out: No such file or directory
```

If you use sudo again within five minutes, it won't ask for your password. Be careful using sudo, since it gives you the ability to modify protected files, all of which are protected to ensure the system runs properly.

Graphical Filesystem Browsers

Because you have the luxury of running Unix within the Mac OS X environment, there's also a terrific graphical way to do some of the things you can do with files from the command line. A *filesystem browser*, such as the Finder, lets you see a graphical representation of the filesystem and do a limited number of operations on it. Figure 2-7 shows the Finder in its default icon view. Other views that are helpful are listing and directory views, each offering more information about the directories above and below the current directory.

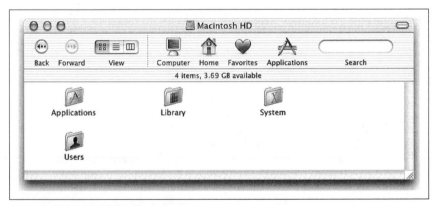

Figure 2-7. Mac OS X Finder, icon view

The Finder can be handy for seeing what's in the filesystem. Unfortunately, because the Finder takes you away from the shell you're using for other work, it can limit what you're able to do with Unix. (You'll see additional information about why this is true when we cover more advanced features such as input/output redirection in Chapter 6.) We recommend learning more about the Finder, but also learning what you can do at the more powerful Unix command line.

CHAPTER 3

File Management

Chapter 2 introduced the Unix filesystem. This chapter explains how to name, edit, copy, move, and find files.

File and Directory Names

As Chapter 2 explained, both files and directories are identified by their names. A directory is really just a special kind of file, so the rules for naming directories are the same as the rules for naming files.

Filenames may contain any character except /, which is reserved as the separator between files and directories in a pathname. Filenames are usually made of upper- and lowercase letters, numbers, "." (dots), and "_" (underscores). Other characters (including spaces) are legal in a filename, but they can be hard to use because the shell gives them special meanings. However, spaces are a standard part of Macintosh file and folder names, so while we recommend using only letters, numbers, dots, and underscore characters for filenames, the reality is that you will have to work with spaces in file and directory names. The Finder, by contrast, dislikes colons (which older versions of Mac OS used as a directory separator, just as Unix uses the slash). If you display a file called *test:me* in the Finder, the name is shown as *test/me* instead. (The reverse is also true: if you create a file in the Finder whose name contains a slash, it will appear as a colon in the Terminal.)

If you have a file with spaces in its name, the shell will be confused if you type its name on the command line. That's because the shell breaks command lines into separate arguments at the spaces. To tell the shell not to break an argument at spaces, either put quotation marks (") around the argument or preface each space with a backslash (\).

For example, the rm program, covered later in this chapter, removes Unix files. To remove a file named *a confusing name*, the first rm command in the following snippet doesn't work, but the second one does. Also note that you can escape spaces (that is, avoid having the shell interpret them inappropriately) by using a backslash character, as shown in the third example:

```
% ls -l
total 2
-rw-r--r--   1 taylor   staff    324 Feb   4 23:07 a confusing name
-rw-r--r--   1 taylor   staff     64 Feb   4 23:07 another odd name
% rm a confusing name
rm: a: no such file or directory
rm: confusing: no such file or directory
rm: name: no such file or directory
% rm "a confusing name"
% rm another\ odd\ name
%
```

You should also use a backslash (\) before any of the following special characters, which have meaning to the shell: * # ` " ' \ $ | & ? ; ~ ( ) < > ! ^.

A filename must be unique inside its directory, but other directories may have files with the same names. For example, you may have the files called *chap1* and *chap2* in the directory */Users/carol/work* and also have different files with the same names in */Users/carol/play*.

File and Directory Wildcards

When you have a number of files named in series (for example, *chap1* to *chap12*) or filenames with common characters (such as *aegis*, *aeon*, and *aerie*), you can use wildcards to specify many files at once. These special characters are * (asterisk), ? (question mark), and [ ] (square brackets). When used in a file or directory name given as an argument on a command line, the following is true:

*   An asterisk stands for any number of characters in a filename. For example, ae* would match *aegis*, *aerie*, *aeon*, etc. if those files were in the same directory. You can use this to save typing for a single filename (for example, al* for *alphabet.txt*) or to choose many files at once (as in ae*). A * by itself matches all file and subdirectory names in a directory, with the exception of any starting with a period. To match all your dot files, try .??*.

?   A question mark stands for any single character (so h?p matches *hop* and *hip*, but not *help*).

[] Square brackets can surround a choice of single characters (i.e., one digit or one letter) you'd like to match. For example, [Cc]hapter would match either *Chapter* or *chapter*, but chap[12] would match *chap1* or *chap2*. Use a hyphen (-) to separate a range of consecutive characters. For example, chap[1-3] would match *chap1*, *chap2*, or *chap3*.

The following examples show the use of wildcards. The first command lists all the entries in a directory, and the rest use wildcards to list just some of the entries. The last one is a little tricky; it matches files whose names contain two (or more) *a*'s.

```
% ls
chap10       chap2        chap5      cold
chap1a.old   chap3.old    chap6      haha
chap1b       chap4        chap7      oldjunk
% ls chap?
chap2    chap5    chap7
chap4    chap6
% ls chap[5-7]
chap5    chap6    chap7
% ls chap[5-9]
chap5    chap6    chap7
% ls chap??
chap10   chap1b
% ls *old
chap1a.old   chap3.old    cold
% ls *a*a*
chap1a.old   haha
```

Wildcards are useful for more than listing files. Most Unix programs accept more than one filename, and you can use wildcards to name multiple files on the command line. For example, both the cat and less programs display files on the screen. cat streams a file's contents until end of file, while less shows the file one screenful at a time. Let's say you want to display files *chap3.old* and *chap1a.old*. Instead of specifying these files individually, you could enter the command as:

```
% less *.old
```

This is equivalent to less chap1a.old chap3.old.

Wildcards match directory names, too. You can use them anywhere in a pathname—absolute or relative—though you still need to separate directory levels with slashes (/). For example, let's say you have subdirectories named *Jan*, *Feb*, *Mar*, and so on. Each has a file named *summary*. You could read all the summary files by typing less */summary. That's almost equivalent to less Jan/summary Feb/summary ... but there's one important difference when you use less */summary: the names will be alphabetized, so *Apr/summary* would be first in the list.

Creating and Editing Files

One easy way to create a file is with a Unix feature called *input/output redirection*, as Chapter 5 explains. This sends the output of a program directly to a file, to make a new file or add to an existing one.

You'll usually create and edit a plain-text file with a text editor program. Text editors are somewhat different than word processors.

Text Editors and Word Processors

A text editor lets you add, change, and rearrange text easily. Three popular Unix editors included with Mac OS X are *vi* (pronounced "vee-eye"), *Pico* ("pea-co"), and *Emacs* ("e-max").

You should choose an editor you're comfortable with. vi is probably the best choice because almost all Unix systems have it, but Emacs is also widely available. If you'll be doing simple editing only, Pico is a great choice. Although Pico is much less powerful than Emacs or vi, it's a lot easier to learn. For this book, however, we'll focus on the rudiments of vi since it's the most widely available Unix editor, and there's a version of vi included with Mac OS X.

None of these plain text editors has the same features as popular word-processing software within the graphical face of Mac OS X, but vi and Emacs are sophisticated, extremely flexible editors for all kinds of plain-text files: programs, email messages, and so on.

Of course, you can opt to use an Aqua-based text editor such as BBEdit or TextEdit with good results too, if you'd rather just sidestep editing while within the Terminal application. If you do, try using the open command within the Terminal to launch the editor with the proper file already loaded. For example: open -e myfile.txt.

By "plain text," we mean a file with only letters, numbers, and punctuation characters in it (text without formatting such as point size, bold and italics, or embedded images). Unix systems use plain-text files in many places: redirected input and output of Unix programs (Chapter 5), as shell setup files (see the section "Customizing Your Shell Environment" in Chapter 4), for shell scripts (shown in the section "Programming" in Chapter 10), for system configuration, and more. Text editors edit these files. When you use a word processor, though, although the screen may look as if the file is only plain text, the file probably also has hidden codes (nontext characters) in it.

Fixing Those Pesky Carriage Returns

The only caveat regarding switching between Aqua (or Classic) applications and Unix applications for editing is that you might end up having to translate file formats along the way. Fortunately, this is easy with Unix.

One of the more awkward things about Apple putting a Mac graphical environment on top of a Unix core is that the two systems use different end-of-line character sequences. If you ever open up a file in an Aqua application and see lots of little boxes at the end of each line, or if you try to edit a file within Unix and find that it's littered with ^M sequences, you've hit the end-of-line problem.

To fix it, use vi to edit *.tcshrc*, the tcsh configuration file:

```
% vi ~/.tcshrc
```

Add the following lines anywhere in the file:

```
alias m2u tr " '\015' '\012' "
alias u2m tr " '\012' '\015' "
```

Save the file, close your current Terminal window, and open a new one. (Each time you launch a new Terminal window, tcsh will process the contents of this file.)

Now, whenever you're working with Unix editing tools and you need to fix a Mac-format file, simply use m2u (Mac to Unix), as in:

```
% m2u < mac-format-file > unix-friendly-file
```

And if you find yourself in the opposite situation, where you're editing a Unix file in a Mac tool and it has some carriage-return weirdness, use the reverse (Unix to Mac) within Terminal before editing:

```
% u2m < unix-friendly-file > mac-format-file
```

Worthy of note is the helpful tr command, which makes it easy to translate all occurrences of one character to another. Use man tr to learn more about this powerful utility.

That's often true even if you tell the word processor to "Save as plain text." One easy way to check for nontext characters in a file is by reading the file with less; look for characters in reversed colors, codes such as <36>, and so on.

If you need to do word processing—making documents, envelopes, and so on—your best bet is to work with a program designed for that purpose such as Microsoft Office X, AppleWorks, or even TextEdit.

The vi Text Editor

The vi editor, originally written by Bill Joy at the University of California, Berkeley, is easy to use once you master the fundamental concept of a modal editor.

Modes can be best explained by thinking about your car stereo. When you have a tape in (or a CD), the "1" button does one task, but if you are listening to the radio, the very same button does something else (perhaps jump to pre-programmed station #1). The vi editor is exactly the same: in *command mode*, i jumps you into insert mode, but in *insert mode* it actually inserts an "i" into the text itself. The handiest key on your keyboard while you're learning vi is unquestionably ESC: if you're in insert mode, ESC will move you back into command mode, and if you're in command mode, it'll beep to let you know that all is well. Use ESC often, until you're completely comfortable keeping track of what mode you're in.

Start vi by typing its name; the argument is the filename you want to create or edit. For instance, to edit your *.tcshrc* setup file, you would cd to your home directory and enter:

```
% vi .tcshrc
```

The terminal fills with a copy of the file (and, because the file is short, some blank lines too, as denoted by the ~ at the beginning of the line), as shown in Figure 3-1.

The bottom row of the window is the status line, which indicates what file you're editing: *.tcshrc: unmodified: line 1*. Quit the program by typing :q and pressing Return while in command mode.

vi tour

Let's take a tour through vi. In this example, you'll make a new file. You can call the file anything you want, but it's best to use only letters and numbers in the filename. For instance, to make a file named *sample*, enter the command vi sample. Let's start our tour now.

1. Your screen should look something like Figure 3-1, but the cursor should be on the top line and the rest of the lines should have the ~ blank line delimiter. Press i to move out of command mode and into insert mode, and you're ready to enter text.

2. Enter some lines of text. Make some lines too short (press Return before the line gets to the right margin). Make others too long; watch how vi wraps long lines. If you have another terminal window open with some text in it or an Aqua application, you can also use your mouse to copy text from another window and paste it into the vi window (always make

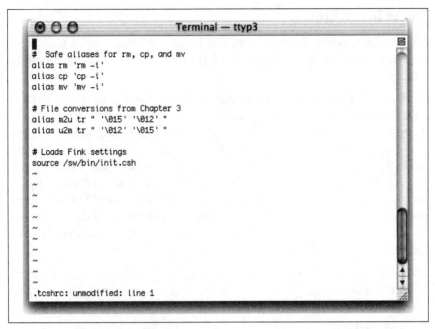

```
  ● ● ●                    Terminal — ttyp3
█
# Safe aliases for rm, cp, and mv
alias rm 'rm -i'
alias cp 'cp -i'
alias mv 'mv -i'

# File conversions from Chapter 3
alias m2u tr " '\015' '\012' "
alias u2m tr " '\012' '\015' "

# Loads Fink settings
source /sw/bin/init.csh
~
~
~
~
~
~
~
~
~
~
.tcshrc: unmodified: line 1
```

Figure 3-1. vi display while editing

sure you're in insert mode before you do this, however, or you could irrevocably mess up your file). To get a lot of text quickly, paste the same text more than once.

3. Let's practice moving around the file. To do this, we'll need to leave insert mode by pressing ESC once. Press it again and you'll hear a beep, reminding you that you are already in command mode. You can use your arrow keys to move around the file, but vi also lets you keep your fingers on the keyboard by using h j k l as the four motion keys (left, down, up, and right, respectively). Unless you have enabled *Option click to position cursor* (see Chapter 4), vi will ignore your mouse if you try to use it to move the cursor. If you've entered a lot of text, you can experiment with various movement commands: H to jump to the first line on the screen, G to jump to the bottom of the file. You should also try the w and b commands, to move forward and backward by words. Also, 0 (zero) jumps to the beginning of the line, while $ jumps to the end.

vi's search or "where is" command, */pattern*, can help you find a word quickly. It's handy even on a short file, where it can be quicker to type / and a word than to use the cursor-moving commands. The search command is also a good example of the way that vi can move your cursor to the status line so you can enter more information. Let's try it by typing /. You should see a display like Figure 3-2.

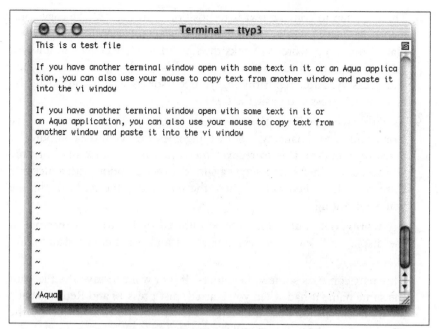

Figure 3-2. vi display while searching

4. Notice that the cursor has jumped to the bottom of the display (which has changed since you started vi) and is sitting next to a /. You can type a word or characters to search for, then press Return to do the search. After a search finishes, you can type n to repeat the search.

5. If your text isn't in paragraphs separated by blank lines, break some of it into paragraphs. Put your cursor at the place you want to break the text and press i to move back into insert mode, then Return twice (once to break the line, another to make a blank line).

6. Now justify one paragraph. Put the cursor at the beginning of the paragraph and type !}fmt. (vi's status line won't change until you press the } character.) Now the paragraph's lines should flow and fit neatly between the margins.

7. Text can be deleted by using x to delete the character that's under the cursor, or the powerful d command: dd deletes lines, dw deletes individual words, d$ deletes to the end of the line, d0 deletes to the beginning of the line, and dG deletes to the end of the file (if you're seeing a pattern and thinking that it's d + *motion specifier* you're absolutely correct). To undo the deletion, press u. You can also paste the deleted text with the p command.

8. The first step to copying text is to position your cursor. The copy command or "yank" works similar to the delete command. The yw command copies one word, yy yanks the line, y1 a single character, and ynw yanks *n* number words. Move the cursor to the line you want to copy and press yy. After repositioning your cursor to where you'd like the text copied, press p to paste the text.

9. As with any text editor, it's a good idea to save your work from vi every 5 or 10 minutes. That way, if something goes wrong on the computer or network, you'll be able to recover the edited buffer since the last time you saved it. When launching vi again, use the -r option with a *filename* to recover the edited buffer where the *filename* is the name of the file you were editing.

   Try writing out your work with :w followed by Return. The bottom of the display will show the filename saved and the number of lines and characters in the file.

   This part confuses some vi beginners. If you want to save the file with the same name it had when you started, just press :w and Return; that's all! You can also choose a different filename: type :w followed by the new filename. Press Return and it's saved.

10. Make one or two more small edits. Then, exit with :q. vi warns you that the file has not been saved. If you want to override the warning type :q!. You can also use a shortcut: :wq writes out your changes and quits vi.

That's it. There's a lot more you can learn about vi, and there's a considerably more sophisticated version of vi called *vim* that you can download for your Mac (*http://www.vim.org/*), if you want something even more powerful. In Table 3-1, you'll find a handy listing of some of the most common vi commands and their descriptions. O'Reilly has two very helpful books if you want to become a power user: *Learning the vi Editor* and *vi Editor Pocket Reference*.

Table 3-1. Common vi editing commands

Command	Meaning
/pattern	Search forward for specified pattern. Repeat search with n.
:q	Quit the edit session.
:q!	Quit, discarding any changes.
:w	Write (save) any changes out to the file.
:wq or ZZ	Write out any changes, then quit (shortcut).
a	Move into append mode (like insert mode, but you enter information after the cursor, not before).
b	Move backward one word.

Table 3-1. Common vi editing commands (continued)

Command	Meaning
w	Move forward one word.
d1G	Delete from the current point back to the beginning of the file.
dd	Delete the current line.
dG	Delete through end of file.
dw	Delete the following word.
ESC	Move into command mode.
h	Move backward one character.
l	Move forward one character.
i	Move into insert mode (ESC moves you back to command mode).
j	Move down one line.
k	Move up one line.
O	Open up a line above the current line and move into insert mode.
o	Open up a line below the current line and move into insert mode.
P	Put (paste) deleted text before the cursor.
p	Put (paste) deleted text after the cursor.
X	Delete character to the left of the cursor.
x	Delete the character under the cursor.
yw	Yank (copy) from the cursor to the end of the current word. You can then paste it with p or P.
yy	Yank (copy) the current line. You can then paste it with p or P.

Managing Your Files

The tree structure of the Unix filesystem makes it easy to organize your files. After you make and edit some files, you may want to copy or move files from one directory to another, or rename files to distinguish different versions of a file. You may want to create new directories each time you start a different project. If you copy a file, it's worth learning about the subtle sophistication of the cp and CpMac commands: if you copy a file to a directory, it automatically reuses the filename in the new location. This can save lots of typing!

A directory tree can get cluttered with old files you don't need. If you don't need a file or a directory, delete it to free storage space on the disk. The following sections explain how to make and remove directories and files.

Creating Directories with mkdir

It's handy to group related files in the same directory. If you were writing a spy novel, you probably wouldn't want your intriguing files mixed with restaurant listings. You could create two directories: one for all the chapters in your novel (*spy*, for example), and another for restaurants (*boston.dine*).

To create a new directory, use the mkdir program. The syntax is:

```
mkdir dirname(s)
```

dirname is the name of the new directory. To make several directories, put a space between each directory name. To continue our example, you would enter:

```
% mkdir spy boston.dine
```

Copying Files

If you're about to edit a file, you may want to save a copy first. That makes it easy to get back the original version. You should use the cp program when copying plain files and directories containing only plain files. Other files having resource forks should be copied with CpMac (available only if you have installed Apple's Mac OS X Developer Tools).

cp

The cp program can put a copy of a file into the same directory or into another directory. cp doesn't affect the original file, so it's a good way to keep an identical backup of a file.

To copy a file, use the command:

```
cp old new
```

where *old* is a pathname to the original file and *new* is the pathname you want for the copy. For example, to copy the */etc/passwd* file into a file called *password* in your working directory, you would enter:

```
% cp /etc/passwd password
%
```

You can also use the form:

```
cp old olddir
```

This puts a copy of the original file *old* into an existing directory *olddir*. The copy will have the same filename as the original.

If there's already a file with the same name as the copy, cp replaces the old file with your new copy. This is handy when you want to replace an old

---

copy with a newer version, but it can cause trouble if you accidentally over-write a copy you wanted to keep. To be safe, use ls to list the directory before you make a copy there. Also, the Mac OS X version of cp has an -i (interactive) option that asks you before overwriting an existing file.

You can copy more than one file at a time to a single directory by listing the pathname of each file you want copied, with the destination directory at the end of the command line. You can use relative or absolute pathnames (see the section "The Mac OS X Filesystem" in Chapter 2) as well as simple file-names. For example, let's say your working directory is /Users/carol (from the filesystem diagram in Figure 2-1). To copy three files called ch1, ch2, and ch3 from /Users/john to a subdirectory called work (that's /Users/carol/work), enter:

```
% cp ../john/ch1 ../john/ch2 ../john/ch3 work
```

Or, you could use wildcards and let the shell find all the appropriate files. This time, let's add the -i option for safety:

```
% cp -i ../john/ch[1-3] work
cp: overwrite work/ch2? n
```

There is already a file named ch2 in the work directory. When cp asks, answer n to prevent copying ch2. Answering y would overwrite the old ch2.

As you saw in the section "Relative pathnames up" in Chapter 2, the short-hand form . puts the copy in the working directory, and .. puts it in the parent directory. For example, the following puts the copies into the work-ing directory:

```
% cp ../john/ch[1-3] .
```

cp can also copy entire directory trees. Use the option -R, for "recursive." There are two arguments after the option: the pathname of the top-level directory you want to copy from and the pathname of the place where you want the top level of the copy to be. As an example, let's say that a new employee, Asha, has joined John and Carol. She needs a copy of John's work directory in her own home directory. See the filesystem diagram in Figure 2-1. Her home directory is /Users/asha. If Asha's own work directory doesn't exist yet (important!), she could type the following commands:

```
% cd /Users
% cp -R john/work asha/work
```

Or, from her home directory, she could have typed cp -R ../john/work work. Either way, she'd now have a new subdirectory /Users/asha/work with a copy of all files and subdirectories from /Users/john/work.

If you give cp -R the wrong pathnames, it can copy a directory tree into itself—running forever until your filesystem fills up!

If the copy seems to be taking a long time, stop cp with Control-Z, then explore the filesystem (ls -RF is handy for this). If all's okay, you can resume the copying by putting the cp job in the background (with bg) so it can finish its slow work. Otherwise, kill cp and do some cleanup—probably with rm -r, which we mention in the section "rmdir" later in this chapter. (Also, see the sections, "Running a Command in the Background" and "Canceling a Process" in Chapter 9.)

Problem checklist

The system says something like "cp: cannot copy file to itself."
If the copy is in the same directory as the original, the filenames must be different.

The system says something like "cp: filename: no such file or directory."
The system can't find the file you want to copy. Check for a typing mistake. If a file isn't in the working directory, be sure to use its pathname.

The system says something like "cp: permission denied."
You may not have permission to copy a file created by someone else or to copy it into a directory that does not belong to you. Use ls -l to find the owner and the permissions for the file, or ls -ld to check the directory. If you feel that you should be able to copy a file, ask the file's owner or use sudo (see "Superuser Privileges with sudo" in Chapter 2) to change its access modes.

The Mac OS X Developer Tools

If you bought the boxed version of Mac OS X, the Developer Tools should be included on a separate CD-ROM. If you bought a new Macintosh that came with Mac OS X preinstalled, the Developer Tools installer will probably be in */Applications/Installers*. Failing either of those, or if you'd like to get the latest version of the tools, they are available to Apple Developer Connection (ADC) members (*http://connect.apple.com/*).

Copying Mac files with resources

The cp program works on plain files and directories, but the Macintosh system stores applications with resource information. These attributes are known as *resource forks*, and are used extensively in Classic Mac OS applications and documents. (You will also find them in various places on the Mac OS X filesystem). A file's resource fork, if it exists, can be seen by looking at a special file called *filename/rsrc*. For example, *Microsoft Word* has a resource fork:

```
% ls -l Microsoft\ Word
-rwxrwxrwx   1 bjepson  admin    10568066 Sep 26 14:26 Microsoft Word
% ls -l Microsoft\ Word/rsrc
-rwxrwxrwx   1 bjepson  admin     2781434 Sep 26 14:26 Microsoft Word/rsrc
```

If you copy *Microsoft Word* with cp, it won't copy the contents of the resource fork (*/tmp* is a directory used to hold temporary files):

```
% cp Microsoft\ Word /tmp
% ls -l /tmp/Microsoft\ Word
-rwxr-xr-x 1 bjepson  wheel  10568066 Nov 10 14:35 /tmp/Microsoft Word
% ls -l /tmp/Microsoft\ Word/rsrc
-rwxr-xr-x 1 bjepson  wheel         0 Nov 10 14:35 /tmp/Microsoft Word/rsrc
```

A special version of cp is used to copy files with resource forks. The program, CpMac, is included with the Mac OS X Developer Tools.

CpMac is found in */Developer/Tools*. To copy *Microsoft Word* and its resources, invoke the following:

```
% /Developer/Tools/CpMac Microsoft\ Word /tmp
% ls -l /tmp/Microsoft\ Word
-rwxrwxrwx 1 bjepson  wheel  10568066 Nov 10 14:37 /tmp/Microsoft Word
% ls -l /tmp/Microsoft\ Word/rsrc
-rwxrwxrwx 1 bjepson  wheel   2781434 Nov 10 14:37 /tmp/Microsoft Word/rsrc
```

 In addition to resource forks, some files may include HFS metadata. A legacy of the earlier Mac OS, HFS metadata holds useful information about a file within the first several bytes of the file itself. The Mac OS X Finder will still make use of some of this data, including creator and type codes that, if a document doesn't have a dot extension such as .mp3, dictate the file's icon as well as which application should launch when you double-click it. A document file that loses this metadata might display only a generic icon, and the Finder wouldn't know which application to launch it with.

Renaming and Moving Files with mv

To rename a file, use mv (move). The mv program can also move a file from one directory to another.

The mv command has the same syntax as the cp command:

```
mv old new
```

old is the old name of the file and *new* is the new name. mv will write over existing files, which is handy for updating old versions of a file. If you don't want to overwrite an old file, be sure that the new name is unique. The Mac OS X version of mv has an -i option for safety:

```
% mv chap1 intro
% mv -i chap2 intro
mv: overwrite `intro'? n
%
```

The previous example changed the file named *chap1* to *intro*, and then tried to do the same with *chap2* (answering n aborted the last operation). If you list your files with ls, you will see that the filename *chap1* has disappeared, but *chap2* and *intro* are preserved.

The mv command can also move a file from one directory to another. As with the cp command, if you want to keep the same filename, you only need to give mv the name of the destination directory.

There's also a MvMac command, analogous to the CpMac command explained earlier. Again, check by looking for a */rsrc* resource file before moving and use MvMac if needed.

If you find yourself using MvMac or CpMac a lot, it'd save you lots of typing to add */Developer/Tools* to your PATH. PATH is one of a set of environment variables that help the shell keep track of your particular session. Information on customizing your path is found in the section "Customizing Your Shell Environment" in Chapter 4.

Finding Files

If your account has lots of files, organizing them into subdirectories can help you find the files later. Sometimes you may not remember which subdirectory has a file. The find program can search for files in many ways; we'll look at two.

Change to your home directory so find will start its search there. Then carefully enter one of the following two find commands. (The syntax is strange and ugly—but find does the job!)

```
% cd
% find . -type f -name "chap*" -print
./chap2
./old/chap10b
% find . -type f -mtime -2 -print
./work/to_do
```

The first command looks in your working directory (.) and all its subdirectories for files (-type f) whose names start with *chap*. (find understands wildcards in filenames. Be sure to put quotes around any filename pattern with a wildcard in it, as we did in the example.) The second command looks for all files that have been created or modified in the last two days (-mtime -2). The relative pathnames that find finds start with a dot (./), the name of the working directory, which you can ignore. Worth noting is that -print displays the results on the screen, not on your printer.

Mac OS X has the 4.4 BSD Unix locate program to find files quickly. You can use locate to search part or all of a filesystem for a file with a certain name.* For instance, if you're looking for a file named *alpha-test*, *alphatest*, or something like that, try this:

```
% locate alpha
/Users/alan/alpha3
/usr/local/projects/mega/alphatest
```

You'll get the absolute pathnames of files and directories with *alpha* in their names. (If you get a lot of output, add a pipe to less. See the section "Piping to a Pager" in Chapter 6.) locate may or may not list protected, private files; its listings usually also aren't completely up to date. The fundamental difference between the two is that find lets you search by file type, contents, and much more, while locate is a simple list of all filenames on the system. To learn much more about find and locate, read your online documentation (see Chapter 10) or read the chapter about them in *Unix Power Tools* (O'Reilly).

Removing Files and Directories

You may have finished work on a file or directory and see no need to keep it, or the contents may be obsolete. Periodically removing unwanted files and directories frees storage space.

rm

The rm program removes files. Unlike moving an item to the trash, no opportunity exists to recover the item before you "empty the trash" when using rm.

The syntax is simple:

```
rm filename(s)
```

---

* The script that updates the locate database is run only once a week (late at night), and your computer must be on and running for that to occur. If you want to update the database by hand, you can use sudo periodic weekly.

rm removes the named files, as the following example shows:

```
% ls
chap10        chap2       chap5    cold
chap1a.old    chap3.old   chap6    haha
chap1b        chap4       chap7    oldjunk
% rm *.old chap10
% ls
chap1b    chap4    chap6    cold    oldjunk
chap2     chap5    chap7    haha
% rm c*
% ls
haha      oldjunk
%
```

When you use wildcards with rm, be sure you're deleting the right files! If
you accidentally remove a file you need, you can't recover it unless you have
a copy in another directory or in your backups.

Do not enter rm * carelessly. It deletes all the files in your
working directory.

Here's another easy mistake to make: you want to enter a
command such as rm c* (remove all filenames starting with
"c") but instead enter rm c * (remove the file named c and
all files!).

It's good practice to list the files with ls before you remove
them. Or, if you use rm's -i (interactive) option, rm asks you
whether you want to remove each file.

rmdir

Just as you can create new directories, you can remove them with the rmdir
program. As a precaution, rmdir won't let you delete directories that contain any files or subdirectories; the directory must first be empty. (The rm -r
command removes a directory and everything in it. It can be dangerous for
beginners, though.)

The syntax is:

```
rmdir dirname(s)
```

If a directory you try to remove does contain files, you get a message like
"rmdir: *dirname* not empty."

To delete a directory that contains some files:

1. Enter cd *dirname* to get into the directory you want to delete.

2. Enter rm * to remove all files in that directory.

3. Enter cd .. to go to the parent directory.

4. Enter rmdir *dirname* to remove the unwanted directory.

Problem checklist

I still get the message "dirname not empty" even after I've deleted all the files.
Use ls -a to check that there are no hidden files (names that start with a period) other than . and .. (the working directory and its parent). The following command is good for cleaning up hidden files (which aren't matched by a simple wildcard such as *). It matches all hidden files except for . (the current directory) and .. (the parent directory):

```
% rm -i .[^.]*
```

Files on Other Operating Systems

Chapter 7 includes the section "Transferring Files," which explains ways to transfer files across a network—possibly to non-Unix operating systems. Mac OS X has the capability of connecting to a variety of different filesystems remotely, including Microsoft Windows, other Unix systems, and even Web-based filesystems.

If the Windows-format filesystem is *mounted* with your other filesystems, you'll be able to use its files by typing a Unix-like pathname. If you've mounted a remote Windows system's *C:* drive over a share named *winc*, you can access the Windows file *C:\WORD\REPORT.DOC* through the pathname */Volumes/winc/word/report.doc*. Indeed, most external volumes are automatically mounted within the */Volumes* directory.

## CHAPTER 4

Customizing Your Session

One of the great pleasures of using Unix with Mac OS X surrounding it is that you get the benefit of a truly wonderful graphical application environment and the underlying power of the raw Unix interface. A match made in heaven!

This chapter discusses how to customize your Terminal environment both from the graphical user interface using Terminal → Window Settings and from the Unix shell by using shell configuration files.

Launching Terminal

Launch Terminal and you have a dull, uninspiring white window with black text that says "Welcome to Darwin!" and a shell prompt. But that's okay. We can fix it.

 By default, Terminal uses tcsh as its shell. If you'd like to configure it to use a different shell, you can do so by selecting Terminal → Preferences and specifying the shell to use.

Changing Terminal Preferences

To change the display preferences in the Terminal application, go to the Terminal menu and choose Window Settings.... You see a display similar to Figure 4-1.

At the top of the window, notice that a drop-down list lets you select which options to configure: Shell, Processes, Emulation, Buffer, Display, Color, and Window. The names suggest what each does, but let's have a closer look anyway, particularly since some of these settings definitely *should* be changed in our view. It's worth pointing out that these changes affect only

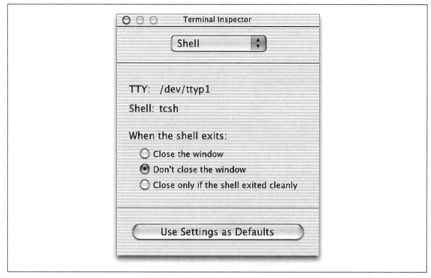

Figure 4-1. Shell Settings

the current window unless you click "Use Settings as Defaults," after which they will apply to all future Terminal windows that you open.

Shell

When you first open Terminal Preferences, the Shell settings are displayed, as shown in Figure 4-1. On this panel you can specify that when a login shell exits, the Terminal application can close the window, close the window only if the shell exited cleanly (that is, returned a nonzero status code, which means that all the applications gracefully shut down), or never close the window. If you like to study what you've done and want to be forced to explicitly close the Terminal window, "Don't close the window" is for you. Otherwise, either of the other two will work fine.

Processes

One of the more subtle capabilities of the Terminal application is that it can keep track of what applications you're running so it can be smart about confirming window close requests: if there's something still running in the window, it'll pop up a dialog box asking if you're sure you want to quit. This feature is very helpful if you are prone to accidentally clicking the wrong window element or pushing the wrong key sequence.

The Processes window shown in Figure 4-2 lists all the processes running under the Terminal window, and lets you specify what to do when you close a window. Set "Prompt before closing window" to Always if you'd like

Terminal to always ask before closing the window or set it to Never to prevent it from ever asking. You can also use "If there are processes other than" setting (the default) to ignore the programs shown in the list (you can add or remove items from this list).

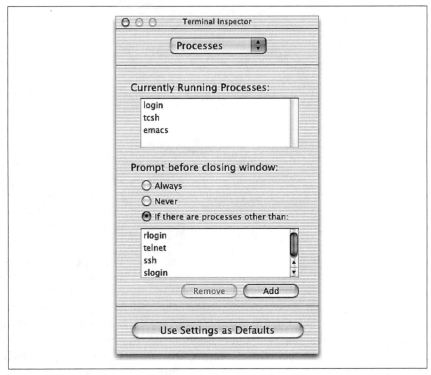

Figure 4-2. Processes

Emulation

These preferences, shown in Figure 4-3, don't need to be altered by most users. If you're using the Emacs text editor, however, you may want to select "Use option key as meta key." What's a meta-key sequence? Emacs uses lots of Control, Alt, Control-Alt, and similar key sequences for complex commands, and one modifier it uses is a new-to-Mac-users "meta" key. If you use Emacs, you'll see when the meta key is necessary. If you don't want to enable this option, you can use the Escape (Esc) key as the meta key for Emacs.

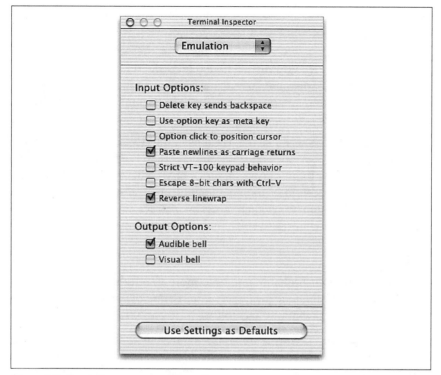

Figure 4-3. Emulation

Some Titanium PowerBook G4s have a long delay before emitting audio, and if you've got one of these and you've noticed it as a problem, deselect "Audible bell" to neatly sidestep the problem. This also has the nice side effect of preventing people around you knowing when you've made a mistake.

Otherwise, it's best to leave "Paste newlines as carriage returns" so that you can ignore the difference in end-of-line sequences in Mac files versus Unix files, and to avoid strict "VT-100" emulation, because it can get in the way of some of the newer Mac OS X Unix utilities. Whether or not you enable "Option click to position cursor" might depend on whether you're a Unix purist (for whom the "good old keyboard" works fine) or whether you're trying to simplify things. Beware that if you do enable Option-Click positioning, it won't work in all cases, only when you're in a full-screen application such as Emacs or vi.

Buffer

The settings in this area probably don't need changing. The scrollback buffer allows you to scroll back and review earlier commands and command output. The default value of 10,000 lines should be more than enough for most people. If you want to use less memory, you can put in a smaller number or completely disable the scrollback buffer, rather than specifying a size.

You can also choose whether the Terminal should wrap long lines (not all Unix programs will wrap long lines, and so they might disappear off the edge of the window if this option isn't set), or whether you should automatically jump to the bottom of the scroll buffer upon input, if you've scrolled back to examine something that transpired earlier in your session. These options are set by default, and you should probably leave them that way.

Display

One area that you'll probably fine tune more than others is Display. Here you can specify a different (or larger) font, define the shape of your cursor within the Terminal window, and control character set encoding.

While you can choose any font available on your system, you'll find that your display is much more comprehensible if you stick to monospace or fixed-width type. Monaco is a very good choice, and is the default typeface for the Terminal application.

Finally, you can specify a nonstandard string encoding if you're working with an unusual language or font. The default UTF-8 (Unicode 8-bit) encoding will work in most situations.

Color

The Color settings let you change the normal text, background, bold text, cursor, and selection colors, as well set the transparency of your Terminal window. The default color settings display black text on a white background, but we find that light text on a dark background is easier to read for extended periods. One suggested setting is to have the background very dark blue, the cursor yellow, normal text light yellow, bold text light green, and the selection dark green.

Window

If you have a large display, or are running at a higher resolution than 800x600, you'll find it quite helpful to enlarge the Terminal window to offer a bigger space within which to work. The default is 80 characters wide by 24 lines tall, as shown in Figure 4-4.

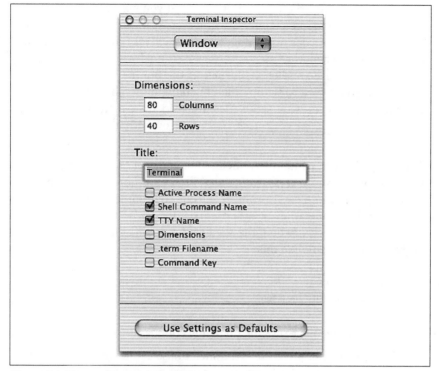

Figure 4-4. Terminal Inspector window

The title of each Terminal window can be fine tuned too: you might find the device name (what you'd get if you typed tty at the shell prompt) and the window dimensions particularly helpful.

> If you want to change the Terminal window title at any point, you can use the Set Title option by either choosing it from the File menu or typing ⌘–Shift-T.

Customizing Your Shell Environment

The Unix shell reads a number of configuration files when it starts up. These configuration files are really *shell programs*, so they are extraordinarily powerful. Shell programming is beyond the scope of this book. For more detail, see Paul DuBois' book *Using csh and tcsh* (O'Reilly). Because Unix is a multiuser system, there are two possible locations for the configuration files: one applies to all users of the system and another to each individual user.

The system-wide setup files that are read by *tcsh*, the default shell for Mac OS X, are found in */etc* (*csh.login*, *csh.cshrc*, and *csh.logout*). You only have permission to change these system-wide files if you use sudo (see "Superuser Privileges with sudo" in Chapter 2). However, you can create an additional file called *.tcshrc* in your home directory that will add additional commands to be executed whenever you start a new Terminal window. (If you configure Terminal to use another shell, such as the Bourne shell, the C shell, or the Z shell, you'll need to set up different configuration files, which we don't discuss.) The system-wide setup files are read first, then the user-specific ones, so commands in your *.tcshrc* file may override those in the system-wide files.

The *.tcshrc* file can contain any shell command that you want to run automatically whenever you create a new Terminal. Some typical examples include changing the shell prompt, setting environment variables (values that control the operation of other Unix utilities), setting aliases, or adding to the search path (where the shell searches for programs to be run). A *.tcshrc* file could look like this:

```
set prompt="%/ %h% "
setenv LESS 'eMq'
alias desktop "cd ~/Desktop"
date
```

This sample *.tcshrc* file issues the following commands:

- The line with set prompt tells the shell to use a different prompt than the standard one. We'll explain the details of prompt setting in the section "Changing Your Prompt" later in this chapter.

- The line with setenv LESS tells the less program which options you want to set every time you use it. Not all commands recognize environment variables, but for those that do, this saves you the trouble of typing the options on every less command line. Environment variables have many uses within Unix. A good place to learn more about them is the book *Unix Power Tools*, by Jerry Peek, Tim O'Reilly, and Mike Loukides (O'Reilly).

- The line that begins with alias defines a new, custom command that your shell will recognize just as if it were a built-in Unix command. Aliases are a great way to save shorthand names for long, complicated Unix command lines, or even to fix common mistakes you might make when typing command lines. This particular alias creates a command for going right to the Desktop directory. We give a brief tutorial on creating aliases later in this chapter.

- The date line simply runs the date command to print the time and date when you open a new Terminal window. You probably don't want to do this, but we want you to understand that you can put in any command that you could type at the shell prompt, and have it automatically executed whenever a new shell starts up.

By default, the *.tcshrc* file doesn't exist in your home directory. Only the system-wide configuration files are read. But if you create the file, it will be read and its contents executed the next time you start a shell. (You can also create a file called *.logout* to contain commands to be executed when you end a shell.) You can create or change these files with a text editor, such as vi (see "The vi Text Editor" in Chapter 3). Don't use a word processor that breaks long lines or puts special nontext codes into the file. Any changes you make to these files will take effect when you open a new Terminal window. Unfortunately, it's not always easy to know which shell setup file you should change.* And an editing mistake in your shell setup file can interfere with the normal startup of the Terminal window. We suggest that beginners get help from experienced users, and don't make changes to these files at all if you're about to do some critical work with your account, unless there's some reason you have to make the changes immediately.

You can execute any customization command we show you here from the command line as well. In this case, the changes are in effect only until you close that window or quit Terminal.

For example, to change the default options for less so it will clear the Terminal window before it shows each new page of text, you could add the -c option to the LESS environment variable. The command would look something like this:

```
% setenv LESS 'eMqc'
```

(If you don't want some of the less options we've shown, you could leave those letters out.) Unix has many other configuration commands to learn about; the sources listed in Chapter 10 can help.

Just as you can execute the setup commands from the command line, the converse is true: any command that you can execute from the command line can be executed automatically when you log in by placing it in your setup file. (Running interactive commands such as vi or ftp from your setup file isn't a good idea, though.)

---

* In addition to *.tcshrc*, the shell will also read and execute files called *.login*, *.cshrc*, and *.logout*. Some files are read by login shells and others by non-login shells. Some are read by subshells, others aren't. Some terminal windows open login shells, others don't. And if you're using the Bourne shell, still other files, such as *.profile*, are read instead. We focus only on *.tcshrc* here, but a more advanced Unix book can provide more information once you need it.

Changing Your Prompt

The easiest customization you can perform is to change your prompt. By default, *tcsh* on Mac OS X has a shell prompt made up of your computer hostname, your account name, and a percent sign (for example: [dsl-132: ~] taylor%). If you'd rather have something else, it's time to edit your own *.tcshrc* file. Use the vi editor (you might need to flip back to "The vi Text Editor" in Chapter 3) to create a file called *.tcshrc* in your home directory (*/Users/yourname*) and add the following to the end of the file: set prompt="% ". You can also change the prompt for a single session by invoking the command as follows:

```
[dsl-132:~]taylor% set prompt="% "
%
```

This command will give you a simple, spare % prompt with nothing else. (The % is traditional for shells derived from the Berkeley Unix C Shell, while $ is traditional for shells derived from the original Bell Labs Bourne Shell.) It's not necessary—you could use a colon, a greater-than sign, or any other prompt character—but it is a nice convention, because it will immediately tell an advanced user what kind of shell you are using.

If that's all you could do to set your prompt, it wouldn't be very interesting, though. There are a number of special character sequences that, when used to define the prompt, cause the shell to print out various bits of useful data. Table 4-1 shows a partial list of these special character sequences for fine tuning your prompt.

Table 4-1. Favorite percent escape sequences for tcsh prompts

Value	Meaning
%/	The current working directory
%~	The current working directory, with your home represented as ~ and other users' homes represented as ~user
%c	The trailing element of the current working directory, with ~ substitution
%h	The current command history number
%M	The full hostname
%m	The hostname up to the first dot
%B/%b	Start/stop bold mode (matches the bold color in the Terminal color preferences)
%t	Time of day in 12-hour (a.m./p.m.) format
%T	Time of day in 24-hour format
%n	The username

Experiment and see what you can create that will meet your needs and be fun too. For many years, a popular Unix prompt was:

```
% set prompt="Yes, Master? "
```

It might be a bit obsequious, but on the other hand, how many people in your life call you "Master"?

One prompt sequence that we like is:

```
% set prompt="%/ %h% "
```

This prompt sequence shows the current working directory, followed by a space, and the current history number, and then a percent sign to remind the user that this is *csh* or *tcsh*. For example, the prompt might read:

```
/Users/taylor 55%
```

This tells me immediately that */Users/taylor* is my current directory, and that I'm on the 55th command I've executed. (Because you can use the arrow keys to scroll back to previous commands, as described in the section, "Recalling Previous Commands" in Chapter 1, this is no longer as important, but there is a very powerful command history syntax built into *tcsh* that allows you to recall a previous command by number. If you're familiar with this syntax, making the command history number part of the prompt can be handy.) On multiuser systems, it's not a bad idea to put the username into the prompt as well, so you always know who the system thinks you are.

Creating Aliases

The flexibility of Unix is simultaneously its greatest strength and downfall; the operating system can do just about anything you can imagine (the command-line interface is certainly far more flexible than Aqua, the graphical interface!) but it's very difficult to remember every single flag to every command. That's where shell aliases can be a real boon. A shell alias is a simple mechanism that lets you create your own command names that act exactly as you desire.

For example, we really like the -a flag to be included every time we list a directory with ls, so we created an alias:

```
% alias ls     "/bin/ls -a"
```

This indicates that each time we type ls in the shell, the /bin/ls command is going to be run, and it's going to automatically have the -a flag specified. To have this available in your next session, make sure you remember to add the alias to your *.tcshrc* file too.

You can also have aliases that let you jump quickly to common locations, a particularly helpful trick when in Mac OS X:

```
% alias desktop "cd ~/Desktop"
```

Chapter 3 described the cp, mv, and rm commands. Each of these support the -i switch, which will prompt you before overwriting or deleting a file. You can use aliases to always enable this switch:

```
% alias rm "rm -i"
% alias cp "cp -i"
% alias mv "mv -i"
```

You can list active aliases all by typing alias without any arguments:

```
% alias
cp        cp -i
desktop   cd ~/Desktop
ls        /bin/ls -a
m2u       (tr '\015' '\012' )
mv        mv -i
rm        rm -i
u2m       (tr '\012' '\015' )
```

Have an alias you really want to omit? You can use unalias for that. For example, unalias ls would remove the -a flag addition.

Setting the Terminal Title

You can change the current Terminal title using the following cryptic sequence of characters:

```
echo '^[]2;My-Window-Title^G'
```

To type the ^[characters in *tcsh*, use the key sequence Control-V Escape (press Control-V and release, then press the Escape key). To type ^G, use Control-V Control-G. The vi editor supports the same key sequence.

Such cryptic sequences of characters are called *ANSI escape sequences*. An ANSI escape sequence is a special command that manipulates some characteristic of the Terminal, such as its title. ^[is the ASCII ESC character (which begins the sequence), and ^G is the ASCII BEL character. (The BEL character is used to ring the Terminal bell, but in this context, it terminates the escape sequence.)

You can capture this escape sequence in a shell alias:

```
% alias settitle 'echo -n "^[]2;\!*^G"'
```

Then you can change the title by issuing this command:

```
% settitle your fancy title here
```

Using AppleScript to Manipulate the Terminal

AppleScript is a powerful programming language used to automate Mac OS X applications. The Mac OS X Terminal is one such application. You can run AppleScript commands at the shell prompt using the osascript utility. The \ character tells the shell that you want to enter a single command on several lines (when you use this, the shell will prompt you with a ? character):

```
osascript -e \
'tell app "Terminal" to set option of first window to value'
```

For example, to minimize your current Terminal window:

```
% osascript -e \
? 'tell app "Terminal" to set miniaturized of first window to true'
%
```

For a complete list of properties you can manipulate with AppleScript, open the Script Editor (*/Applications/AppleScript*) and select File → Open Dictionary. Open the Terminal dictionary and examine the properties available under *window*. If a property is marked [r/o], it is read-only, which means you can't modify it on the fly.

Further Customization

There's not much more you can do with the Terminal application than what's shown in this chapter, but there's an infinite amount of customization possible with the *tcsh* shell (or any other shell you might have picked). To learn more about how to customize your shell, read the manpage. Be warned, though, the *tcsh* manpage is over 4,700 lines long!

Oh, and in case you're wondering, manpages are the Unix version of online help documentation. Just about every command-line (Unix) command has a corresponding manpage with lots of information on starting flags, behaviors, and much more. You can access any manpage by simply typing man *cmd*. Start with man man to learn more about the man system.

For more information on customizing *tcsh*, see Paul DuBois' book, *Using csh and tcsh*, or *Unix Power Tools*, by Jerry Peek, Tim O'Reilly, and Mike Loukides, both available from O'Reilly.

CHAPTER 5

Printing

Working in the Macintosh environment, you're used to a simple and elegant printer interface, particularly in Mac OS X, where Print Center makes it a breeze to add new printers and configure your existing printers. Until the advent of the Common Unix Printing System (CUPS), the Unix environment has never had a printing interface that even comes close in usability. As of Mac OS X 10.2, Print Center and CUPS are combined in a way that brings joy to command-line and GUI lovers alike.

 When you add a printer with Print Center, you'll only see some of the printer models that Mac OS X and CUPS support. To get access to advanced options, including extra print drivers, hold down the Option key when you click the Add button. To get even more printer drivers, download and install the Mac OS X release of gimp-print (*http://gimp-print. sourceforge.net/*). The gimp-print release is available as a disk image that includes a graphical installer.

Formatting and Print Commands

Before you print a file on a Unix system, you may want to reformat it to adjust the margins, highlight some words, and so on. Most files can also be printed without reformatting, but the raw printout might not look quite as nice. Further, some printers accept only PostScript, which means you'll need to use a text-to-PostScript filter such as enscript for good results. Before we cover printing itself, let's look at both pr and enscript to see how they work.

pr

The pr program does minor formatting of files on the terminal screen or for a printer. For example, if you have a long list of names in a file, you can format it onscreen into two or more columns.

PostScript is a page description language supported by some printer models. PostScript printers were once the norm among Macintosh users, and still are popular. If you're using an inexpensive inkjet printer or a low- to mid-range laser printer, chances are good that your printer doesn't support PostScript. Some of the utilities described in this section require PostScript, others don't.

The syntax is:

```
pr option(s) filename(s)
```

pr changes the format of the file only on the screen or on the printed copy; it doesn't modify the original file. Table 5-1 lists some pr options.

Table 5-1. Some pr options

Option	Description
-k	Produces k columns of output
-d	Double-spaces the output
-h header	Prints header at top of each page
-t	Eliminates printing of header and top/bottom margins

Other options allow you to specify the width of columns, set the page length, etc. For a complete list of options, see the manpage, man pr.

Before using pr, here are the contents of a sample file named *food*:

```
% cat food
Sweet Tooth
Bangkok Wok
Mandalay
Afghani Cuisine
Isle of Java
Big Apple Deli
Sushi and Sashimi
Tio Pepe's Peppers
%
```

Let's use pr options to make a two-column report with the header "Restaurants":

```
% pr -2 -h "Restaurants" food

Feb  4  9:58 2002  Restaurants    Page 1

Sweet Tooth            Isle of Java
Bangkok Wok            Big Apple Deli
Mandalay               Sushi and Sashimi
```

```
Afghani Cuisine        Tio Pepe's Peppers
.
.
.
%
```

The text is output in two-column pages. The top of each page has the date and time, header (or name of the file, if a header is not supplied), and page number. To send this output to the default Mac OS X printer instead of to the terminal screen, create a pipe to the lpr printer program:

```
% pr -2 -h "Restaurants" food | lpr
```

See the section "Pipes and Filters" in Chapter 6 for more information on pipes.

pr does not require a PostScript printer.

enscript

One reason for the success of the Macintosh has been its integrated support of PostScript for printing. Allowing sophisticated imaging and high-quality text, PostScript printers are quite the norm in the Mac world. However, this proves a bit of a problem from the Unix perspective, because Unix commands are used to working with regular text without any special PostScript formatting included.

Translating plain text into PostScript is the job of enscript. The enscript program has a remarkable number of different command flags, allowing you access to all the layout and configuration options you're familiar with from the Page Setup and Print dialog boxes in Aqua.

The most helpful command flags are summarized in Table 5-2 (you can learn about all the many options to enscript by reading the enscript manpage). A typical usage is enscript -p - Sample.txt | lpr to send the file to a printer or enscript -psample.ps sample.txt to output to the file *sample.ps*.

Table 5-2. Useful enscript options

Option	Description
-B	Do not print page headers.
-f *font*	Print body text using *font* (the default is Courier10).
-j	Print borders around columns (you can turn on multicolumn output with -1 or -2).
-p *file*	Send output to *file*. Use - to stream output to standard out (for pipes).
-r	Rotate printout 90 degrees, printing in landscape mode instead of portrait (the default).
-W *lang*	Output in the specified language. Default is PostScript, but enscript also supports HTML, overstrike, and RTF.

enscript requires a PostScript printer.

lpr

The other possibility for printing is the standard Unix command lpr for sending files to your default printer (as chosen using Print Center). The syntax is:

    lpr option(s) filename(s)

After you enter the command to print a file, the shell prompt returns to the screen and you can enter another command. However, seeing the prompt doesn't mean your file has been printed. Your file has been added to the printer queue to be printed in turn.

To print a file named *bills* on the default printer, use the lpr command, as in this example:

    % **lpr bills**
    %

lpr has no output if everything was accepted and queued properly. If you need ID numbers for lpr jobs, use the lpq program to view the print queue (see the section "lpq" later in this chapter). The file *bills* will be sent to the default system printer. lpr has several options. Table 5-3 lists three of them.

Table 5-3. Some lpr options

Command	Description
-Pprinter	Use given printer name if there is more than one printer at your site. The printer names are assigned in Print Center.
-#	Print # copies of the file.
-m	Notify sender by email when printing is done.

Problem checklist

lpr returns "jobs queued, but cannot start daemon."

Your system is probably not configured properly for an lpr printer. If you have a named lpr printer that works, try the command again with the -Pprintername option. If not, you might want to try using atprint or opening up your files in TextEdit and printing from the Aqua environment.

My printout hasn't come out.

See whether the printer is printing now. If it is, other users may have made requests to the same printer ahead of you, and your file should be printed in turn. The following section explains how to check the print requests.

If no file is printing, check the printer's paper supply, physical connections, and power switch. The printer may also be hung (stalled). If it is, ask other users or system staff people for advice.

My printout is garbled or doesn't look anything like the file did on my terminal.
The printer may not be configured to handle the kind of file you're printing. For instance, a file in plain-text format will look fine when previewed in your Terminal window, but look like gibberish when you try to print it. If the printer understands only PostScript, make sure that you use enscript to translate the plain-text format into acceptable PostScript.

lpr does not require a PostScript printer.

Viewing the Printer Queue

If you want to find out how many files or "requests" for output are ahead of yours in the printer queue, use the program named lpq. The lprm command lets you cancel print jobs from the lpr queue.

Remember that you can also check on the status of print jobs by going into Applications → Utilities → Print Center. Double-click on the printer to see the state of the queue.

lpq

The lpq command shows what's currently printing and what's in the queue for the default printer:

```
% lpq
Office_Jet is ready and printing
Rank    Owner   Job    File(s)                              Total Size
active  taylor 11      12.tiff                              923648 bytes
1st     taylor 12      Slashdot: News for nerds, stuff 231424 bytes
%
```

The first line displays the printer status. If the printer is disabled or out of paper, you may see different messages on this first line. Here you can see that the printer is ready for new print jobs, and is currently printing. Jobs are printed in the order indicated in the lpq output. The Job number is important, because you can remove print jobs from the queue (if you're the owner) with lprm.

lprm

lprm terminates lpr requests. You can specify either the ID of the request (displayed by lpq) or the name of the printer.

If you don't have the request ID, get it from lpq, then use lprm. Specifying the request ID cancels the request, even if it is currently printing:

```
% lprm 8
```

To cancel whatever request is currently printing, regardless of its ID, simply enter lprm and the printer name:

```
% lprm
```

lprm does not provide any feedback unless it encounters an error.

atprint

If you have an AppleTalk printer, there is a set of easy-to-use AppleTalk-aware Unix commands included with Mac OS X. The most important of the commands is atprint, which lets you easily stream any Unix output to a printer.

To start working with the AppleTalk tools, run atlookup, which lists all the AppleTalk devices recognized on the network (and that can be quite a few):

```
% atlookup
Found 4 entries in zone *
ff1d.a0.80      Dave Taylor's Computer:Darwin
ff01.04.08      PET:SNMP Agent
ff01.04.9d      PET:LaserWriter
ff01.04.9e      PET:LaserJet 2100
```

You can see that the PET printer (an HP LaserJet2100) appears with two different AppleTalk addresses. Fortunately, that can safely be ignored as well as the other AppleTalk devices that show up in the list. The important thing is that the atlookup command confirmed that there is indeed an AppleTalk printer online.

To select a specific AppleTalk printer as the default printer for the atprint command, run the oddly named at_cho_prn command. The trick is that you need to run this command as *root* or administrator. Use the sudo command (see "Superuser Privileges with sudo" in Chapter 2) to run the program as *root*:

```
% sudo at_cho_prn
Password:
  1: ff01.04.9dtPET:LaserWriter

ITEM number (0 to make no selection)?1
Default printer is:PET:LaserWriter@*
status: idle
```

(If you are on a multi-zone network, you'll be prompted to select a zone.) Now, finally, the PET printer is selected as the default AppleTalk printer, and all subsequent invocations of `atprint` will be sent to that printer without having to remember its exact name.

Because most of the printers available through AppleTalk on a Macintosh network are PostScript printers, it's essential to use the `enscript` program to ensure the output is in proper PostScript format. As an example, the following prints the intro manpage (an introduction to the manpage system) on the PET printer, properly translated into PostScript:

```
% man intro | enscript -p - | atprint
man: Formatting manual page...
Looking for PET:LaserWriter@*.
Trying to connect to PET:LaserWriter@*.
[ 1 pages * 1 copy ] left in -
atprint: printing on PET:LaserWriter@*.
```

Pipes (command sequences with | between the commands) are covered in more detail in Chapter 6.

`atprint` does not require a PostScript printer (unless used with `enscript`), but it does require an AppleTalk printer.

Non-PostScript Printers

The `lpr` command can handle a variety of file types, including PDF, plain text, and a variety of image types (JPEG, TIFF, and others). If your printer does not support PostScript, you will not be able to use `lpr` to print PostScript files directly. This also means that you won't be able to use `enscript` for printing.

However, if you've installed Fink (see "Fink" in Chapter 8), you can install the ghostscript package and run `ps2pdf` to turn your PostScript file into a PDF. To run `enscript` on the *food* file, convert it to PDF, and print it, use pipes between `enscript`, `ps2pdf`, and `lpr`:

```
% enscript -o - food | ps2pdf - - | lpr
```

The `-o` - switches and the pipe symbol (|) tell `enscript` to send its PostScript output to the `ps2pdf` program. The - - options and the pipe tell `ps2pdf` to read its input from the pipe and send its output to `lpr`, which sends the PDF to the printer. For more information on pipes, see Chapter 6.

Redirecting I/O

Many Unix programs read input (such as a file) and write output. In this chapter, we discuss Unix programs that handle their input and output in a standard way. This lets them work with each other.

This chapter generally *doesn't* apply to full-screen programs, such as the vi editor, that take control of your whole Terminal window. (The pager programs, less, and more do work together in this way.) It also doesn't apply to graphical programs, such as the Finder or Internet Explorer, that open their own windows on your screen.

Standard Input and Standard Output

What happens if you don't give a filename argument on a command line? Most programs will take their input from your keyboard instead (after you press Return to start the program running, that is). Your Terminal keyboard is the program's *standard input.*

As a program runs, the results are usually displayed on your Terminal screen. The Terminal screen is the program's *standard output.* So, by default, each of these programs takes its information from the standard input and sends the results to the standard output. These two default cases of input/output (I/O) can be varied. This is called *I/O redirection.*

If a program doesn't normally read from files, but reads from its standard input, you can give a filename by using the < (less-than symbol) operator. tr (character translator) is such a program. Here's how to use the input redirection operator to convert commas to linefeeds in the *to_do* file:

```
% cat to_do
Install Mac OS X,Learn Unix,???,Profit!
% tr ',' '\n' < to_do
Install Mac OS X
```

```
Learn Unix
???
Profit!
%
```

If a program writes to its standard output, which is normally the screen, you can make it write to a file instead by using the greater-than symbol (>) operator. The pipe operator (|) sends the standard output of one program to the standard input of another program. Input/output redirection is one of the most powerful and flexible Unix features.

Putting Text in a File

Instead of always letting a program's output come to the screen, you can redirect output to a file. This is useful when you'd like to save program output, or when you put files together to make a bigger file.

cat

cat, which is short for "concatenate," reads files and outputs their contents one after another, without stopping.

To display files on the standard output (your screen), use:

```
cat file(s)
```

For example, let's display the contents of the file */etc/csh.login*. This system file is the global login file for *tcsh* and *csh*.

```
% cat /etc/csh.login
# System-wide .login file for csh(1).

setenv PATH "/bin:/sbin:/usr/bin:/usr/sbin"
%
```

You cannot go back to view the previous screens, as you can when you use a pager program such as less (unless you're using a Terminal window with a sufficient scrollback buffer, that is). cat is mainly used with redirection, as we'll see in a moment.

By the way, if you enter cat without a filename, it tries to read from the keyboard (as we mention earlier). You can get out by pressing Control-D.

When you add > *filename* to the end of a command line, the program's output is diverted from the standard output to the named file. The > symbol is called the *output redirection operator*.

When you use the > operator, be careful not to accidentally overwrite a file's contents. Your system may let you redirect output to an existing file. If so, the old file will be deleted (or, in Unix lingo, "clobbered"). Be careful not to overwrite a much needed file!

Many shells can protect you from this risk. In the *tcsh* shell (the default shell for Mac OS X), use the command set noclobber. Enter the command at a shell prompt or put it in your *.tcshrc* file. After that, the shell won't allow you to redirect onto an existing file and overwrite its contents.

This doesn't protect against overwriting by Unix programs such as cp; it works only with the > redirection operator. For more protection, you can set Unix file access permissions.

For example, let's use cat with the output redirection operator. The file contents that you'd normally see on the screen (from the standard output) are diverted into another file, which we'll then read using cat (without any redirection!):

```
% cat /etc/csh.login > mylogin
% cat mylogin
# System-wide .login file for csh(1).

setenv PATH "/bin:/sbin:/usr/bin:/usr/sbin"
%
```

An earlier example showed how cat /etc/csh.login displays the file */etc/csh. login* on the screen. The example here adds the > operator, so the output of cat goes to a file called *mylogin* in the working directory. Displaying the file *mylogin* shows that its contents are the same as the file */etc/csh.login* (the effect is the same as the copy command cp /etc/csh.login mylogin).

You can use the > redirection operator with any program that sends text to its standard output—not just with cat. For example:

```
% who > users
% date > today
% ls
mylogin    today    users    ...
```

We've sent the output of who to a file called *users* and the output of date to the file named *today*. Listing the directory shows the two new files. Let's look at the output from the who and date programs by reading these two files with cat:

```
% cat users
taylor    console  Nov 11 22:06
taylor    ttyp1    Nov 15 08:16
% cat today
Fri Nov 15 17:11:00 EST 2002
%
```

You can also use the cat program and the > operator to make a small text file. We told you earlier to type Control-D if you accidentally enter cat without a filename. This is because the cat program alone takes whatever you type on the keyboard as input. Thus, the command:

```
cat > filename
```

takes input from the keyboard and redirects it to a file. Try the following example:

```
% cat > to_do
Finish report by noon
Lunch with Xian
Swim at 5:30
^D
%
```

cat takes the text that you typed as input (in this example, the three lines that begin with Finish, Lunch, and Swim), and the > operator redirects it to a file called *to_do*. Type Control-D *once*, on a new line by itself, to signal the end of the text. You should get a shell prompt.

You can also create a bigger file from smaller files with the cat command and the > operator. The form:

```
cat file1 file2 > newfile
```

creates a file *newfile*, consisting of *file1* followed by *file2*.

```
% cat today to_do > diary
% cat diary
Fri Nov 15 17:11:00 EST 2002
Finish report by noon
Lunch with Xian
Swim at 5:30
%
```

 You shouldn't use redirection to add a file to itself, along with other files. For example, you might hope that the following command would merge today's to-do list with tomorrow's. This won't work!

```
% cat to_do to_do.tomorrow > to_do.tomorrow
```

It works, but it runs for all eternity because it keeps copying the file over itself. If you cancel it with Control-C and use ls to examine the file, you'll see that it's gotten quite large:

```
^C
% ls -sk to_do.tomorrow
 81704 to_do.tomorrow
```

ls -sk shows the size in kilobytes, so it grew to about 80 megabytes! The right way to do this is by using a temporary file (as you'll see in a later example) or simply by using a text editor program.

You can add more text to the end of an existing file, instead of replacing its contents, by using the >> (append redirection) operator. Use it as you would the > (output redirection) operator. So:

```
cat file2 >> file1
```

appends the contents of *file2* to the end of *file1*. For an example, let's append the contents of the file *users* and the current date and time to the file *diary*. Here's what it looks like:

```
% cat users >> diary
% date >> diary
% cat diary
Fri Nov 15 17:11:00 EST 2002
Finish report by noon
Lunch with Xian
Swim at 5:30
taylor    console  Nov 11 22:06
taylor    ttyp1    Nov 15 08:16
Fri Nov 15 17:53:24 EST 2002
%
```

Unix doesn't have a redirection operator that adds text to the beginning of a file. You can do this by storing the new text in a temporary file, then by using a text editor program to read the temporary file into the start of the file you want to edit. You also can do the job with a temporary file and redirection. Maybe you'd like each day's entry to go at the beginning of your *diary* file. Simply rename *diary* to something like *temp*. Make a new *diary* file with today's entries, then append *temp* (with its old contents) to the new *diary*. For example:*

```
% mv diary temp
% date > diary
% cat users >> diary
% cat temp >> diary
% rm temp
```

Pipes and Filters

We've seen how to redirect input from a file and output to a file. You can also connect two *programs* together so that the output from one program becomes the input of the next program. Two or more programs connected in this way form a *pipe*. To make a pipe, put a vertical bar (|) on the command line between two commands. When a pipe is set up between two

---

* This example could be shortened by combining the two cat commands into one, giving both filenames as arguments to a single cat command. That wouldn't work, though, if you were making a real diary with a command other than cat users.

commands, the standard output of the command to the left of the pipe symbol becomes the standard input of the command to the right of the pipe symbol. Any two commands can form a pipe as long as the first program writes to standard output and the second program reads from standard input.

When a program takes its input from another program, performs some operation on that input, and writes the result to the standard output (which may be piped to yet another program), it is referred to as a *filter*. A common use of filters is to modify output. Just as a common filter culls unwanted items, Unix filters can restructure output.

Most Unix programs can be used to form pipes. Some programs that are commonly used as filters are described in the next sections. Note that these programs aren't used only as filters or parts of pipes. They're also useful on their own.

grep

The grep program searches a file or files for lines that have a certain pattern. The syntax is:

```
grep "pattern" file(s)
```

The name "grep" is derived from the ed (a Unix line editor) command g/re/p, which means "globally search for a regular expression and print all matching lines containing it." A *regular expression* is either some plain text (a word, for example) and/or special characters used for pattern matching. When you learn more about regular expressions, you can use them to specify complex patterns of text.

The simplest use of grep is to look for a pattern consisting of a single word. It can be used in a pipe so only those lines of the input files containing a given string are sent to the standard output. But let's start with an example reading from files: searching all files in the working directory for a word—say, *Unix*. We'll use the wildcard * to quickly give grep all filenames in the directory.

```
% grep "Unix" *
ch01:Unix is a flexible and powerful operating system
ch01:When the Unix designers started work, little did
ch05:What can we do with Unix?
%
```

When grep searches multiple files, it shows the filename where it finds each matching line of text. Alternatively, if you don't give grep a filename to read, it reads its standard input; that's the way all filter programs work:

```
% ls -l | grep "Jan"
drwx------    4 taylor  staff    264 Jan 29 22:33 Movies/
drwx------    2 taylor  staff    264 Jan 13 10:02 Music/
drwxr-xr-x   12 root    staff    364 Jan  9 20:24 NetInfo/
drwx------   95 taylor  staff   3186 Jan 29 22:44 Pictures/
drwxr-xr-x    3 taylor  staff    264 Jan 24 21:24 Public/
%
```

First, the example runs ls -l to list your directory. The standard output of ls -l is piped to grep, which only outputs lines that contain the string Jan (that is, files or directories that were last modified in January and any other lines that have the pattern "Jan" within). Because the standard output of grep isn't redirected, those lines go to the Terminal screen.

grep options let you modify the search. Table 6-1 lists some of the options.

Table 6-1. Some grep options

Option	Description
-v	Print all lines that do not match pattern.
-n	Print the matched line and its line number.
-l	Print only the names of files with matching lines (lowercase letter "L").
-c	Print only the count of matching lines.
-i	Match either upper- or lowercase.

Next, let's use a regular expression that tells grep to find lines with *root*, followed by zero or more other characters (abbreviated in a regular expression as .*), then followed by Jan:*

```
% ls -l | grep "root.*Jan"
drwxr-xr-x   12 root    staff    364 Jan  9 20:24 NetInfo/
%
```

For more about regular expressions, see the references in the section "Documentation" in Chapter 10.

sort

The sort program arranges lines of text alphabetically or numerically. The following example sorts the lines in the *food* file (from the section "pr" in

---

* Note that the regular expression for "zero or more characters," .*, is different than the corresponding filename wildcard *. See the section "File and Directory Wildcards" in Chapter 3. We can't cover regular expressions in enough depth here to explain the difference, though more-detailed books do. As a rule of thumb, remember that the first argument to grep is a regular expression; other arguments, if any, are filenames that can use wildcards.

Chapter 5) alphabetically. sort doesn't modify the file itself; it reads the file and writes the sorted text to the standard output.

```
% sort food
Afghani Cuisine
Bangkok Wok
Big Apple Deli
Isle of Java
Mandalay
Sushi and Sashimi
Sweet Tooth
Tio Pepe's Peppers
```

By default, sort arranges lines of text alphabetically. Many options control the sorting, and Table 6-2 lists some of them.

Table 6-2. Some sort options

Option	Description
-n	Sort numerically (example: 10 sorts after 2); ignore blanks and tabs.
-r	Reverse the sorting order.
-f	Sort upper- and lowercase together.
+x	Ignore first *x* fields when sorting.

More than two commands may be linked up into a pipe. Taking a previous pipe example using grep, we can further sort the files modified in January by order of size. The following pipe uses the commands ls, grep, and sort:

```
% ls -l | grep "Jan" | sort +4n
drwx------    2 taylor  staff    264 Jan 13 10:02 Music/
drwx------    4 taylor  staff    264 Jan 29 22:33 Movies/
drwxr-xr-x    3 taylor  staff    264 Jan 24 21:24 Public/
drwxr-xr-x   12 root    staff    364 Jan  9 20:24 NetInfo/
drwx------   95 taylor  staff   3186 Jan 29 22:44 Pictures/
%
```

This pipe sorts all files in your directory modified in January by order of size, and prints them to the Terminal screen. The sort option +4n skips four fields (fields are separated by blanks), then sorts the lines in numeric order. So, the output of ls, filtered by grep, is sorted by the file size (this is the fifth column, starting with 1605). Both grep and sort are used here as filters to modify the output of the ls -l command. You could print the listing by piping the sort output to your printer command (either lp, lpr, or atprint).

Piping to a Pager

The less program, which you saw in the section "Looking Inside Files with less" in Chapter 2, can also be used as a filter. A long output normally zips by you on the screen, but if you run text through less, the display stops after each screenful of text.

Let's assume that you have a long directory listing. (If you want to try this example and need a directory with lots of files, use cd first to change to a system directory such as /bin or /usr/bin.) To make it easier to read the sorted listing, pipe the output through less:

```
% ls -l | grep "Jan" | sort +4n | less
drwx------   2 taylor  staff    264 Jan 13 10:02 Music/
drwx------   4 taylor  staff    264 Jan 29 22:33 Movies/
drwxr-xr-x   3 taylor  staff    264 Jan 24 21:24 Public/
drwxr-xr-x  12 root    staff    364 Jan  9 20:24 NetInfo/
  .
  .
  .
drwx------  95 taylor  staff   3186 Jan 29 22:44 Pictures/
:
```

less reads a screenful of text from the pipe (consisting of lines sorted by order of file size), then prints a colon (:) prompt. At the prompt, you can type a less command to move through the sorted text. less reads more text from the pipe and shows it to you and saves a copy of what it has read, so you can go backward to reread previous text if you want. (The simpler pager program more can't back up while reading from a pipe.) When you're done seeing the sorted text, the q command quits less.

Exercise: Redirecting Input/Output

In the following exercises you redirect output, create a simple pipe, and use filters to modify output.

Task	Command
Redirect output to a file.	ls > files
Change all the letters to uppercase.	tr '[a-z]' '[A-Z]' < files
Sort the output of a program.	ls | sort
Append sorted output to a file.	ls | sort >> files
Display output to the screen.	less files (or more files)
Display long output to the screen.	ls -l /bin | less (or more)
Format and print a file with pr.	pr files | lp or pr files | lpr

## CHAPTER 7

Accessing the Internet

A network lets computers communicate with each other, sharing files, email, and much more. Unix systems have been networked for more than 25 years, and Macintosh systems have always had networking as an integral part of the system design from the very first system released in 1984.

This chapter introduces Unix networking: remotely accessing your Mac from other computers and copying files between computers.

Remote Logins

There may be times when you need to access your Mac, but you can't get to the desk it's sitting on. If you're working on a different computer, you may not have the time or inclination to stop what you're doing, walk over to your Mac, and log in (laziness may not be the only reason for this: perhaps someone else is using your Mac when you need to get on it or perhaps your Mac is miles away). Mac OS X's file sharing (System Preferences → Sharing) can let you access your files, but there may be times you want to use the computer interactively, perhaps to move files around, search for a particular file, or perform a system maintenance task.

If you enable Remote Login under System Preferences → Sharing, you can access your Mac's Unix shell from any networked computer that can run SSH (*http://www.ssh.com*), OpenSSH (*http://www.openssh.org*), or a compatible application such as PuTTY (a Windows implementation of SSH available at *http://www.chiark.greenend.org.uk/~sgtatham/putty/*). SSH and OpenSSH can be installed on many Unix systems, and OpenSSH is included with many Linux distributions as well as Mac OS X.

Figure 7-1 shows how remote login programs such as ssh work. In a local login, you interact directly with the shell program running on your local system. In a remote login, you run a remote-access program on your local system; that program lets you interact with a shell program on the remote system.

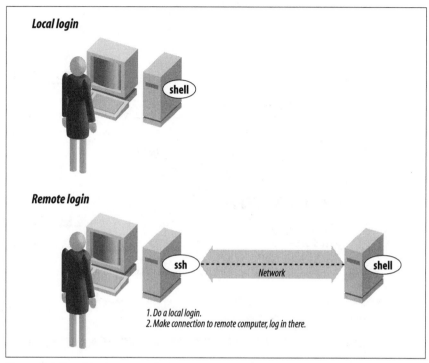

Figure 7-1. Local login, remote login

When you enable Remote Login, the Sharing panel will display instructions for logging into your Mac from another computer. This message is shown in Figure 7-2.

To log in to your Mac from a remote Unix system, use the command shown in the Sharing panel, as shown in the following sample session (the first time you connect, you'll be asked to vouch for your Mac's authenticity):

```
Last login: Sun Nov 17 21:21:37 2002 from 192.168.254.182
Sun Microsystems Inc.   SunOS 5.9      Generic May 2002
bash-2.05$ ssh bjepson@192.168.254.182
The authenticity of host '192.168.254.182' can't be established.
RSA key fingerprint in md5 is:
0a:9c:48:8c:9d:d1:b7:18:1b:3b:02:4a:dd:02:72:2a
Are you sure you want to continue connecting(yes/no)?yes
Warning: Permanently added '192.168.254.182' (RSA) to the list
of known hosts.
```

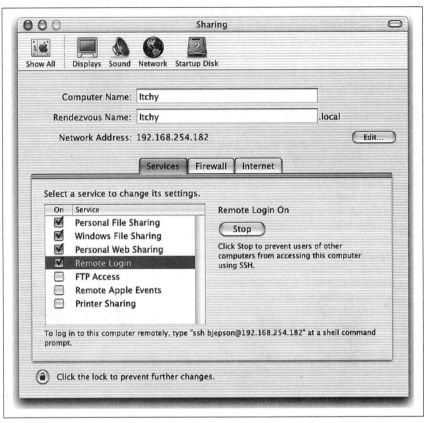

Figure 7-2. Instructions for remote access to your Mac

```
bjepson@192.168.254.182's password:
Last login: Sun Nov 17 21:04:30 2002
Welcome to Darwin!
%
```

To log in to your Mac from a Windows machine using PuTTY, launch the PuTTY application, specify SSH (the default is to use the Telnet protocol described later), and type in your Mac OS X system's IP address as shown in the Mac's Sharing panel. PuTTY will prompt you for your Mac OS X username and password. Figure 7-3 shows a sample PuTTY session.

Web and FTP Access

You can also use the Sharing preferences panel to enable your system's Web and FTP server. Start Personal Web Sharing to enable the Web server. Other users can access the main home page (located in */Library/WebServer/Documents*) using *http://address*, where *address* is your machine's IP address or

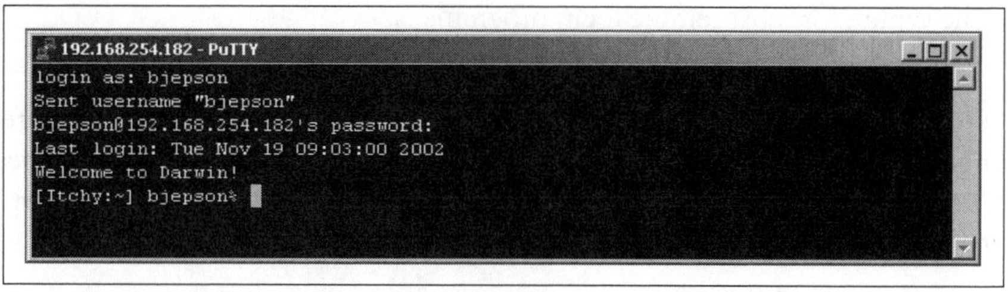

Figure 7-3. Connecting to Mac OS X with PuTTY

host name (see the sidebar "Remote Access and the Outside World" if you are using an Airport Base Station or other router between your network and the Internet).

Remote Access and the Outside World

If your Macintosh has an IP address that was assigned by an Airport Base Station, then it's very likely that your machine will not be visible to the outside world. Because of this, you will only be able to connect to your Mac from machines on your network. You can allow remote users to connect by using the Airport Admin Utility's Port Mapping tab (for Remote Login via ssh, you must map port 22 to your Macintosh; use port 80 for Personal Web Sharing). Other SOHO (Small Office/Home Office) gateways may support this feature as well.

If you use this technique, the IP address shown on the Sharing panel will be incorrect. You should use your Airport Base Station's WAN address when you connect from a computer outside your network.

Start FTP Access to enable remote users to use FTP to connect to your system. Again, remote users should use your machine's IP address or hostname to connect.

Remote Access to Other Unix Systems

You can also connect to other systems from Mac OS X. To do so, launch the Terminal application. Then start a program that connects to the remote computer. In addition to ssh, some typical programs for connecting over a computer network are telnet, rsh (remote shell), or rlogin (remote login). All of these are supported and included with Mac OS X. In any case, when you log off the remote computer, the remote login program quits and you get another shell prompt from your Mac.

The syntax for most remote login programs is:

```
program-name remote-hostname
```

For example, when Dr. Nelson wants to connect to the remote computer named *biolab.medu.edu*, she'd first make a local login to her Mac named *fuzzy* by launching Terminal. Next, she'd use the telnet program to reach the remote computer. Her session would look something like this:

```
Welcome to Darwin!
fuzzy% telnet biolab.medu.edu

Medical University Biology Laboratory

biolab.medu.edu login: jdnelson
Password:

biolab$
.
.
.
biolab$ exit
Connection closed by foreign host.
fuzzy%
```

Her accounts have shell prompts that include the hostname. This reminds her when she's logged in remotely. If you use more than one system but don't have the hostname in your prompt, see the sections "Changing Your Prompt" in Chapter 4 or "Documentation" in Chapter 10 to find out how to add it.

 When you're logged on to a remote system, keep in mind that the commands you type will take effect on the remote system, not your local one! For instance, if you use lpr to print a file, the printer it comes out of may be very far away.

The programs rsh (also called rlogin) and ssh generally don't give you a login: prompt. These programs assume that your remote username is the same as your local username. If they're different, give your remote username on the command line of the remote login program, as shown in the next example.

You may be able to log in without typing your remote password or passphrase.* Otherwise, you'll be prompted after entering the command line.

---

* In ssh, you can run an *agent* program, such as ssh-agent, that asks for your passphrase once, then handles authentication every time you run ssh or scp afterward.

Following are four sample ssh and rsh command lines. The first pair shows how to log in to the remote system, *biolab.medu.edu*, when your username is the same on both the local and remote systems. The second pair shows how to log in if your remote username is different (in this case, *jdnelson*); note that the Mac OS X versions of ssh and rsh may support both syntaxes shown depending on how the remote host is configured:

```
% ssh biolab.medu.edu
% rsh biolab.medu.edu
% ssh jdnelson@biolab.medu.edu
% rsh -l jdnelson biolab.medu.edu
```

About Security

Today's Internet and other public networks have users who try to break into computers and snoop on other network users. While the popular media calls these people *hackers*, most hackers are self-respecting programmers who enjoy pushing the envelope of technology. These evildoers are better known as *crackers*. Most remote login programs (and file transfer programs, which we cover later in this chapter) were designed 20 years ago or more, when networks were friendly places with cooperative users. Those programs (many versions of telnet and rsh, for instance) make a cracker's job easy. They transmit your data across the network in a way that allows even the most inexperienced crackers to read it, and they either send your password along, visible to the crackers. Worse, some of these utilities can be configured to allow access without passwords.

SSH is different; it was designed with security in mind. It sends your password (and everything else transmitted or received during your SSH session) in a secure way. A good place to get more details on SSH is the book *SSH: The Secure Shell*, by Daniel J. Barrett and Richard Silverman (O'Reilly).

Transferring Files

You may need to copy files between computers. For instance, you can put a backup copy of an important file you're editing onto an account at a computer in another building or another city. Dr. Nelson could put a copy of a datafile from her local computer onto a central computer, where her colleagues can access it. Or you might want to download 20 files from an FTP server, but not want to go through the tedious process of clicking on them one by one in a web browser window. If you need to do this sort of thing often, you may be able to set up a networked filesystem connection; then you'll be able to use the Finder or local programs such as cp and mv. But Unix systems also have command-line tools for transferring files between computers. These often work more quickly than graphical tools. We explore them later in this section.

scp and rcp

Mac OS X includes both scp (secure copy) and rcp (remote copy) programs for copying files between two computers. In general, you must have accounts on both computers to use these. The syntax of scp and rcp are similar to cp, but also let you add the remote hostname to the start of a file or directory pathname. The syntax of each argument is:

> *hostname:pathname*

hostname: is needed only for remote files. You can copy from a remote computer to the local computer, from the local computer to a remote computer, or between two remote computers.

The scp program is much more secure than rcp, so we suggest using scp to transfer private files over insecure networks such as the Internet. For privacy, scp encrypts the file and your passphrase.

For example, let's copy the files *report.may* and *report.june* from your home directory on the computer named *giraffe.intuitive.com* and put the copies into your working directory (.) on the machine you're presently logged in to. If you haven't set up the SSH agent that lets you use scp without typing your passphrase, scp will ask you:

```
% scp giraffe.intuitive.com:report.may giraffe.intuitive.com:report.june .
Enter passphrase for RSA key 'taylor@mac':
```

To use wildcards in the remote filenames, put quotation marks ("*name*") around each remote name.* You can use absolute or relative pathnames; if you use relative pathnames, they start from your home directory on the remote system. For example, to copy all files from your *food/lunch* subdirectory on your *giraffe* account into your working directory (.) on the local account, enter:

```
% scp "giraffe.intuitive.com:food/lunch/*" .
```

Unlike cp, the Mac OS X versions of scp and rcp don't have an -i safety option. If the files you're copying already exist on the destination system (in the previous example, that's your local machine), those files are overwritten.

---

* Quotes tell the local shell not to interpret special characters, such as wildcards, in the filename. The wildcards are passed, unquoted, to the remote shell, which interprets them *there*.

If your system has rcp, your system administrator may not want you to use it for system security reasons. Another program, ftp, is more flexible and secure than rcp (but much less secure than scp).

FTP

FTP, or file transfer protocol, is a standard way to transfer files between two computers. Many users of earlier Mac OS versions are familiar with Fetch (*http://fetchsoftworks.com/*), a shareware graphical FTP client that runs on Mac OS X as well as earlier versions.

The Unix ftp program does FTP transfers from the command line. There are also a number of easy-to-use graphical FTP tools available from the Apple web site (go to Get Mac OS X Software... from the Apple menu and click on Internet Utilities). But we cover the standard ftp program here. The computers on either end of the FTP connection must be connected by a network (such as the Internet).

To start FTP, identify yourself to the remote computer by giving the username and password for your account on that remote system. Unfortunately, sending your username and password over a public network means that snoopers might see them—and use them to log into your account on that system.

A special kind of FTP, *anonymous FTP*, happens if you log in to the remote server with the username *anonymous*. The password is your email address, such as *alex@foo.co.uk*. (The password isn't usually required; it's a courtesy to the remote server.) Anonymous FTP lets anyone log in to a remote system and download publicly accessible files to their local systems.

Command-line ftp

To start the standard Unix ftp program, provide the remote computer's hostname:

```
ftp hostname
```

ftp prompts for your username and password on the remote computer. This is something like a remote login (see the section "Remote Logins," earlier in this chapter), but ftp doesn't start your usual shell. Instead, ftp prints its own prompt and uses a special set of commands for transferring files. Table 7-1 lists the most important ftp commands.

Table 7-1. Some ftp commands

Command	Description
put *filename*	Copies the file *filename* from your local computer to the remote computer. If you give a second argument, the remote copy will have that name.
mput *filenames*	Copies the named files (you can use wildcards) from the local computer to the remote computer.
get *filename*	Copies the file *filename* from the remote computer to your local computer. If you give a second argument, the local copy will have that name.
mget *filenames*	Copies the named files (you can use wildcards) from the remote computer to the local computer.
prompt	A "toggle" command that turns prompting on or off during transfers with the mget and mput commands. By default, mget and mput will prompt you "mget *filename*?" or "mput *filename*?" before transferring each file; you answer y or n each time. Typing prompt once, from an ftp> prompt, stops the prompting; all files will be transferred without question until the end of the ftp session. Or, if prompting is off, typing prompt at an ftp> prompt resumes prompting.
cd *pathname*	Changes the working directory on the remote machine to *pathname* (ftp typically starts at your home directory on the remote machine).
lcd *pathname*	Changes ftp's working directory on the local machine to *pathname*. (ftp's first local working directory is the same working directory from which you started the program.) Note that the ftp lcd command changes only ftp's working directory. After you quit ftp, your shell's working directory will not have changed.
dir	Lists the remote directory (like ls -l).
binary	Tells ftp to copy the file(s) that follow it without translation. This preserves pictures, sound, or other data.
ascii	Transfers plain-text files, translating data if needed. For instance, during transfers between a Microsoft Windows system (which adds Control-M to the end of each line of text) and a Unix system (which doesn't), an ascii-mode transfer removes or adds those characters as needed.
passive	Toggles the setting of passive mode. This may help ftp to run correctly if you are behind a firewall. If you put the command setenv FTP_PASSIVE 1 in your *.tcshrc*, all your ftp sessions will use passive mode.
quit	Ends the ftp session and takes you back to a shell prompt.

Here's an example. Carol uses ftp to copy the file *todo* from her *work* subdirectory on her account on the remote computer *rhino*:

```
% ls
afile    ch2    somefile
% ftp rhino.zoo.edu
Connected to rhino.zoo.edu.
Name (rhino:carol): csmith
Password:
ftp> cd work
ftp> dir
total 3
-rw-r--r--  1 csmith   mgmt     47 Feb  5  2001 for.ed
```

```
-rw-r--r--  1 csmith    mgmt    264 Oct 11 12:18 message
-rw-r--r--  1 csmith    mgmt    724 Nov 20 14:53 todo
ftp> get todo
ftp> quit
% ls
afile   ch2    somefile    todo
```

We've explored the most basic ftp commands here. Entering help at an ftp> prompt gives a list of all commands; entering help followed by an ftp command name gives a one-line summary of that command.

SFTP: FTP to secure sites

If you can only use ssh to connect to a remote site, chances are it won't support regular FTP transactions either, probably due to higher security. Mac OS X also includes a version of ftp that works with the standard SSH server programs and works identically to regular FTP. Just type sftp at the command line.

FTP with a web browser

If you need a file from a remote site, and you don't need all the control that you get with the ftp program, you can use a web browser to download files using anonymous FTP. To do that, make a URL (location) with this syntax:

```
ftp://hostname/pathname
```

For instance, *ftp://somecorp.za/pub/reports/2001.pdf* specifies the file *2001.pdf* from the directory */pub/reports* on the host *somecorp.za*. In most cases, you can also start with just the first part of the URL—such as *ftp://somecorp.za*— and browse your way through the FTP directory tree to find what you want. If your web browser doesn't prompt you to save a file, use its Save menu command.

An even faster way to download a file is with the curl (copy from URL) command. For example, to save a copy of the report in the current directory, simply enter:

```
% curl -O ftp://somecorp.za/pub/reports/2001.pdf
```

Without the -O option, curl will display the file in the Terminal window. If you want to read a text file from an Internet server, you can combine curl and less:

```
% curl ftp://ftp.oreilly.com/pub/README.ftp | less
```

You can also use curl with web pages, but this will bring the page up in HTML source view (to read HTML documents from the Terminal, see "Lynx, a Text-Based Web Browser" in Chapter 8):

```
% curl http://www.oreilly.com | less
```

The wget utility is available through Fink (see "Fink" in Chapter 8). With wget, you can download individual files. The following example saves the O'Reilly home page to *index.html*:

```
% wget http://www.oreilly.com
```

You can also mirror web sites to your local system with the -r option (the mirrored web site is saved in a subdirectory of your current directory):

```
% wget -r http://www.oreilly.com
```

Use caution with the -r option, since it can use a lot of bandwidth and take up a lot of disk space. For more information about wget, read its manpage with the command man wget.

Other FTP solutions

One of the pleasures of working with Unix within the Mac OS X environment is that there are a wealth of great Aqua applications. In the world of FTP-based file transfer, the choices are all uniformly excellent, starting with *Fetch*, *NetFinder*, *rbrowser*, and *Anarchie*, and encompassing many other possibilities. Again, either open the Apple menu and select "Get Mac OS X Software..." or try VersionTracker (*http://www.versiontracker.com/*), Mac OS X Apps (*http://www.macosxapps.com/*), MacUpdate (*http://macupdate.com/*) or the shareware archive site Download.com (*http://www.download.com/*).

Practice

You can practice your ftp skills by connecting to the public FTP archive *ftp.apple.com*. Log in as *ftp* with your email address as the password, then look around. Try downloading a research paper or document. If you have an account on a remote system, try using rcp and scp to copy files back and forth.

## CHAPTER 8

Unix-Based Internet Tools

If you're going to be interacting with the Internet extensively, odds are good that you'll opt for attractive and easy-to-use Aqua applications. Bear with us, though; there's a lot of power in the Unix command-line alternatives, and they're well worth learning.

Fink

The Fink Project is made up of volunteers who are bringing open source software to Mac OS X. They do the work that is needed to make these programs run smoothly and keep them updated so they work with the latest release of Mac OS X.

Two of the programs featured in this chapter, Lynx and Pine, are available through Fink, as is a wealth of other applications. To install Fink, do the following:

1. Download the binary installer disk image (a *.dmg* file) from *http://fink.sourceforge.net/download*.

2. In the Finder, double-click the *.dmg* file to mount the disk image.

3. Open the mounted disk image and double-click the Fink Installer *.pkg* package inside.

4. Follow the instructions on the screen.

 You can also find an installer for Lynx and Pine by selecting the "Get Mac OS X Software..." menu from the Apple menu, which opens a web browser and takes you to the Apple web site. From there, find and click on the "Unix & Open Source" link, which offers a list of useful Unix applications, including Lynx and Pine. The advantage of using Fink is that it will manage thousands of available packages, making sure that you have the latest versions and that different packages cooperate with each other.

To begin using Fink, you need to set up your PATH and some environment variables. Fink provides a shell script to help with this. Add this command to your *.tcshrc* file (see "The vi Text Editor" in Chapter 3):

```
source /sw/bin/init.csh
```

Next, close your Terminal window and open a new one. You won't notice anything different, but the addition of the command will configure future Terminal sessions for Fink. After you've installed Fink and started a new Terminal session, you can use the apt-get utility to install Lynx and Pine. When you issue the apt-get command, you must use sudo (see "Superuser Privileges with sudo" in Chapter 2) so you can make changes to the system.

Installing Packages

After you've done a fresh install of Fink, you must update the list of available packages with apt-get update (you should also run this command every couple of weeks to see if any new packages have been released):

```
% sudo apt-get update
Password:
Get:1 http://us.dl.sourceforge.net release/main Packages [112kB]
Get:2 http://us.dl.sourceforge.net release/main Release [85B]
Get:3 http://us.dl.sourceforge.net release/crypto Packages [9247B]
Get:4 http://us.dl.sourceforge.net release/crypto Release [87B]
Get:5 http://us.dl.sourceforge.net current/main Packages [112kB]
Get:6 http://us.dl.sourceforge.net current/main Release [85B]
Get:7 http://us.dl.sourceforge.net current/crypto Packages [9247B]
Get:8 http://us.dl.sourceforge.net current/crypto Release [87B]
Fetched 243kB in 1s (207kB/s)
Reading Package Lists... Done
Building Dependency Tree... Done
```

After you've done this, you can use the apt-get install command to install Lynx:

```
% sudo apt-get install lynx
Reading Package Lists... Done
Building Dependency Tree... Done
The following NEW packages will be installed:
  lynx
0 packages upgraded, 1 newly installed, 0 to remove and 0  not upgraded.
Need to get 1319kB of archives. After unpacking 0B will be used.
Get:1 http://us.dl.sourceforge.net release/main lynx 2.8.4-1 [1319kB]
Fetched 1319kB in 11s (120kB/s)
Selecting previously deselected package lynx.
(Reading database ... 3450 files and directories currently installed.)
Unpacking lynx (from .../lynx_2.8.4-1_darwin-powerpc.deb) ...
Setting up lynx (2.8.4-1) ...
```

http://finkcommander.sourceforge.net/ is home to FinkCommander, a free graphical user interface for Fink. Use this program if you'd rather have an Aqua interface to maintain your Fink installation.

When you use apt-get to install a package, Fink searches a web site for a pre-built package provided by the volunteers. A pre-built package is an application that has been bundled up in a manner similar to the installers used by other Mac OS X applications. As of this writing, there was no binary package for Pine. However, if you've installed the Mac OS X Developer Tools (see "The Mac OS X Developer Tools" in Chapter 3), you can use the fink install command to automatically download, compile, and install an application:

```
% fink install pine
sudo /sw/bin/fink  install pine
Password:
Information about 1710 packages read in 3 seconds.

pkg pine  version ###
pkg pine  version 4.44-2
The following package will be installed or updated:
 pine
[... output deleted for brevity ...]
```

The fink install command performs a lot of actions on your behalf: downloading source code, locating patches (modifications to the source code that provide Mac OS X compatibility), compiling the source, and installing the compiled programs. This process can take a long time, depending on which packages you have selected. If you select a package that depends on another package, fink will automatically install it. If there are many dependencies between packages, you could be in for a long wait.

For this reason, it's best to use apt-get to install packages whenever possible. Since apt-get uses precompiled packages, you don't have to download all the source and wait for compilation. Also, apt-get warns you if there are any dependencies, and gives you a chance to abort:

```
% sudo apt-get install ethereal
Password:
Reading Package Lists... Done
Building Dependency Tree... Done
The following extra packages will be installed:
   dlcompat glib glib-shlibs gtk+ gtk+-data gtk+-shlibs libpcap
   libpcap-shlibs system-xfree86 zlib
The following NEW packages will be installed:
   dlcompat ethereal glib glib-shlibs gtk+ gtk+-data gtk+-shlibs
   libpcap libpcap-shlibs system-xfree86 zlib
```

```
0 packages upgraded, 11 newly installed, 0 to remove and 0  not upgraded.
Need to get 13.7MB of archives. After unpacking 0B will be used.
Do you want to continue? [Y/n]
```

Listing Available Packages

To see a list of available packages, use the command fink list (this sample
shows an abbreviated list):

```
% fink list
Information about 1710 packages read in 1 seconds.

      3dpong        0.4-2       Pong clone
      a2ps          4.12-4      Any to PostScript filter
   i  aalib         1.4rc5-2    Ascii art library
   i  aalib-bin     1.4rc5-2    Ascii art library
   i  aalib-shlibs  1.4rc5-2    Ascii art library
      abiword       1.0.2-2     Open-source word processor
```

An i in the leftmost column indicates that the package is already installed.
The second column is the package name to use with apt-get install. The
third column shows the version number, and the last column provides a
description of the package.

Lynx, a Text-Based Web Browser

There are a number of excellent web browsers available for Mac OS X,
including Microsoft Internet Explorer, Chimera, Mozilla, Omniweb, and
Opera. However, attractive, graphically based web browsers can be slow—
especially with flashy, graphics-laden web pages on a slow network.

The Lynx web browser (originally from the University of Kansas, and available on many Unix systems) is different because it's a text-based web
browser that works within the Terminal application. Being text-only causes
it to have some tradeoffs you should know about. Lynx indicates where
graphics occur in a page layout; you won't see the graphics, but the bits of
text that Lynx uses in their place can clutter the screen. Still, because it
doesn't have to download or display those graphics, Lynx is *fast*, which is
especially helpful over a dialup modem or busy network connection. Sites
with complex multicolumn layouts can be hard to follow with Lynx; a good
rule is to page through the screens, looking for the link you want and ignore
the rest. Forms and drop-down lists are a challenge at first, but Lynx always
gives you helpful hints for forms and lists, as well as other web page ele-
ments, in the third line from the bottom of the screen. With those warts
(and others), though, once you get a feel for Lynx you may find yourself
choosing to use it—even on a graphical system.

The Lynx command line syntax is:

```
lynx "location"
```

For example, to visit the O'Reilly home page, enter lynx "http://www.
oreilly.com" or simply lynx "www.oreilly.com". (It's safest to put quotes
around the location, because many URLs have special characters that the
shell might interpret otherwise.) Figure 8-1 shows part of the home page.

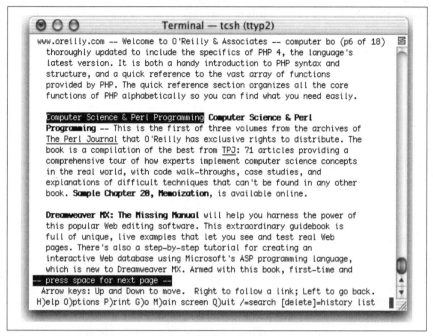

Figure 8-1. Lynx display

To move around the Web, Lynx uses your keyboard's arrow keys, spacebar,
and a set of single-letter commands. The third line from the bottom of a
Lynx screen gives you a hint of what you might want to do at the moment.
In Figure 8-1, for instance, "press space for next page" means you can see
the next screenful of this web page by pressing the spacebar (at the bottom
edge of your keyboard). Lynx doesn't use a scrollbar; instead, use the spacebar to go forward in a page, and use the b command to move back to the
previous screenful of the same web page. The bottom two lines of the screen
remind you of common commands, and the help system (which you get by
typing h) lists the rest.

The links (which you would click on if you were using a graphical web
browser) are highlighted. One of those links is the *currently selected link*,
which you can think of as the link where your cursor sits. Depending on

how you've configured Terminal, links are either boldfaced or presented in a different color, and the selected link (in Figure 8-1, that's the first: "Computer Science & Perl Programming") is in reverse video.

When you first view a screen, the link nearest the top is selected. Figure 8-2 shows what you can do at a selected link. To select a later link (farther down the page), press the down-arrow key. The up-arrow key selects the previous link (farther up the page). Once you've selected a link you want to visit, press the right-arrow key to follow that link; the new page appears. Go back to the previous page by pressing the left-arrow key (from any selected link; it doesn't matter which one).

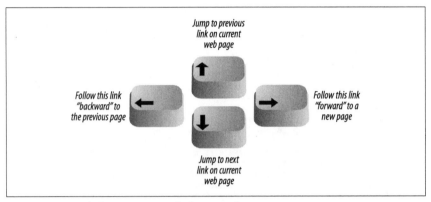

Figure 8-2. Lynx link navigation with the arrow keys

Although Lynx can't display graphics in the Terminal (*no* program can!), it will let you download links that point to graphical files. Then you can use Aqua programs—such as Preview —to view or print those files.

There's much more to Lynx; type H for an overview. Lynx command-line options let you configure almost everything. For a list of options, type man lynx (see the section "Documentation" in Chapter 10) or use:

```
% lynx -help | less
```

Electronic Mail with Pine

When you install Mac OS X or boot it for the first time, the installer may ask whether you want to sign up for .Mac, Apple's suite of Internet services that includes *electronic mail* (email). If you signed up for .Mac, you probably use Apple's Mail application to send and receive email. If you didn't sign up for .Mac, you may be using an email account provided by your Internet Service Provider (ISP) or employer along with Apple's Mail or some other application.

There are many great graphical mail applications for Mac OS X. However, Terminal-based email programs have some benefits:

- They are often faster than graphically-rich email applications because their displays are so much simpler.
- They can be faster to use because your fingers don't need to leave the keyboard.
- They are not affected by conventional email viruses, although security holes do appear from time to time in nearly every program that interacts with the Internet.
- You can read your email while logged in to your Mac from another machine (see "Remote Logins" in Chapter 7).

Pine, from the University of Washington, is a popular program for reading and sending email from a terminal. It works completely from your keyboard; you don't need a mouse. This section describes how to configure Pine and use it to send and receive email.

Start Pine by entering its name at a shell prompt. It also accepts options and arguments on its command line; to find out more, enter pine -h (help). Figure 8-3 shows the starting display, the *main menu*.

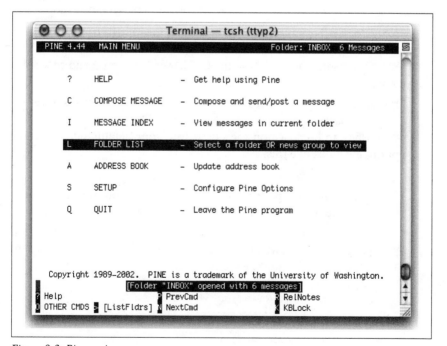

Figure 8-3. Pine main menu

Configuring Pine

The Pine main menu has a Setup entry for configuring Pine. After you enter S (the "Setup" command), you can choose what kind of setup you want. From the setup screen, you can get to the option configuration area with C (the "Config" command).

The configuration screen has page after page of options. You can look through them with the spacebar (to move forward one page), the - key (back one page), the N key (to move forward to the next entry), and the P key (back to the previous entry). If you know the name of an option you want to change, you can search for it with W (the "Whereis" command).

When you highlight an option, the menu of commands at the bottom of the screen will show you what can do with that particular option. A good choice, while you're exploring, is the ? (help) command, to find out about the option you've highlighted. There are several kinds of options:

- Options with variable values: names of files, hostnames of computers, and so on. For example, the personal-name option sets the name used in the "From:" header field of mail messages you send. The setup entry looks like this:

      personal-name   = <No Value Set: using "Robert L. Stevenson">

  "No Value Set" can mean that Pine is using the default from the system-wide settings, as it is here. If this user wants his email to come from "Bob Stevenson," he could use the C (Change Val) command to set that name.

- Options that set preferences for various parts of Pine. For instance, the enable-sigdashes option in the "Composer Preferences" section puts two dashes and a space on the line before your default signature. The option line looks like this:

      [X] enable-sigdashes

  The X means that this preference is set, or "on." If you want to turn this option off, use the X (Set/Unset) command to toggle the setting.

- Options for which you can choose one of many possible settings. The option appears as a series of lines. For instance, the first few lines of the saved-msg-name-rule option look like this:

      saved-msg-name-rule   =
                Set   Rule Values
                ---   ----------------------
                (*)   by-from
                ( )   by-nick-of-from
                ( )   by-nick-of-from-then-from
                ( )   by-fcc-of-from
                ( )   by-fcc-of-from-then-from

The * means that the `saved-msg-name-rule` option is currently set to by-from. (Messages will be saved to a folder named for the person who sent the message.) If you wanted to choose a different setting—for instance, `by-fcc-of-from`—you'd move the highlight to that line and use the * (Select) command to choose that setting.

These settings are trickier than the others, but the built-in help command ? explains each choice in detail. Start by highlighting the option name (here, `saved-msg-name-rule`) and reading its help info. Then look through the settings' names, highlight one you might want, and read its help info to see if it's right for you.

When you exit the setup screen with the E command, Pine asks you to confirm whether you want to save any option changes you made. Answer N if you were just experimenting or aren't sure.

Configuring Pine to send and receive email

Before you can send or receive email with Pine, you must configure it to talk to your email servers. You will need the following information (if you are not using .Mac, you will need to get this information from your ISP or system administrator):

Your email address
This will be supplied by your ISP. If you are using .Mac, it will be `username@mac.com`.

Your Mac OS X username must be the same as the username in your email address, since Pine uses your Mac OS X username and your *user-domain* to generate your email address.

Incoming mail server
This is the server where your email messages sit until you're ready to read them. Your ISP may refer to this as a POP or IMAP server. If you are using .Mac, this will be `mail.mac.com`.

Incoming mail protocol
Pine supports two protocols for downloading remote email: POP (Post Office Protocol) and IMAP (Internet Message Access Protocol). If you are using .Mac, this will be IMAP.

Outgoing mail server
This is a server that accepts your outgoing email and delivers it to the recipients. Your ISP may refer to this as an SMTP server (SMTP is Simple Mail Transfer Protocol, the network protocol for sending and receiving email). If you are using .Mac, this will be `smtp.mac.com`.

Enter the setup screen by pressing S at Pine's main menu. Then press C to enter the Config screen. To configure your email account, do the following:

1. Look at your email address. Set Pine's *user-domain* to everything after the @ symbol (for example, mac.com).

2. Set the *smtp-server* to your outgoing mail server (for example, smtp.mac.com).

3. Set your *inbox-path*:

    a. If you are using IMAP, set the inbox-path to {*incoming mail server/*user=*username*}inbox, as in {mail.mac.com/user=dtaylor}inbox.

    b. If you are using POP, set the inbox-path to {*incoming mail server/*pop3/user=*username*}inbox, as in {pop3.nowhere.oreilly.com/pop3/user=dtaylor}inbox.

The exact settings may vary. If you need more help, visit the Usenet newsgroup *comp.mail.pine* and look for the latest posting of the FAQ (see "Usenet News," later in this chapter).

After you've made these changes, press E to exit Setup, press Y to commit changes, and then quit and restart Pine.

Reading Email with Pine

When you first start Pine, the main menu appears, as shown earlier in Figure 8-3. You may also be prompted for your password, since Pine needs this to connect to your POP or IMAP server.

The highlighted line, which is the default command, gives a list of your email folders.* You can choose the highlighted command by pressing Return, pressing the greater-than sign >, or typing the letter next to it. (Here, this is 1—a lowercase L. You don't need to type the commands in uppercase.) But because you probably haven't used Pine before, the only interesting folder is the inbox, which is the folder where your new messages wait for you to read them.

The display in Figure 8-3 shows that there are six messages waiting. Let's go directly to the inbox by pressing I (or by highlighting that line in the menu and pressing Return) to read the new mail. Figure 8-4 has the *message index* for our inbox.

---

* Pine also lets you read Usenet newsgroups. The L command takes you to another display where you choose the source of the folders, *then* you see the list of folders from that source. See the section "Usenet News."

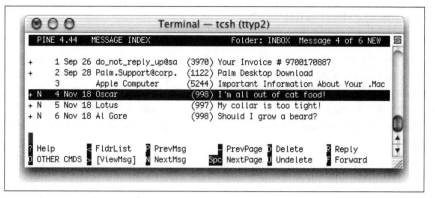

Figure 8-4. Pine message index

The main part of the window is a list of the messages in the folder, one message per line. If a line starts with N, as the fourth message does, it's a new message that hasn't been read. (The first message has been sitting in the inbox for some time now.) Next on each line is the *message number*; messages in a folder are numbered 1, 2, and so on. That's followed by the date the message was sent, who sent it, the number of characters in the message (size), and, finally, the message subject.

At the bottom of the display is Pine's reminder list of commands. When you aren't sure what to do, this is a good place to look. If you don't see what you want here, pressing O (the letter "o"; lowercase is fine) shows you more choices. For more information, ? gives detailed help.

Let's skip the first few messages and read number 4. The down-arrow key or the N key moves the highlight bar over that message. As usual, you can get the default action—the one shown in brackets at the bottom of the display (here, [ViewMsg])—by pressing Return or >. The message from Oscar will appear.

Just as > takes you forward in Pine, the < key generally takes you back to where you came from—in this case, the message index. You can type R to reply to this message, F to forward it (send it on to someone else), D to mark it for deletion, and the Tab key to go to the next message without deleting this one.

When you mark a message for deletion, it stays in the folder message index, marked with a D at the left side of its line, until you quit Pine. Type Q to quit. Pine asks if you really want to quit. If you've marked messages for deletion, Pine asks if you want to *expunge* ("really delete") them. Answering Y here deletes the message.

Sending Email with Pine

If you've already started Pine, you can compose a message from many of its displays by typing C. (Though, as always, not every Pine command is available at every display.) You can also start from the main menu. Or, at a shell prompt, you can go straight into message composition by typing pine *addr1 addr2*, where each *addr* is an email address such as *jerry@oreilly.com*. In that case, after you've sent the mail message, Pine quits and leaves you at another shell prompt.

When you compose a message, Pine puts you in a window called the *composer*. (You'll also go into the composer if you use the Reply or Forward commands while you're reading another mail message.) The composer is a lot like another Unix text editor (Pico), but the first few lines are special because they're the message *header*—the "To:," "Cc:" (courtesy copy), "Attchmnt:" (attached file), and "Subject:" lines. Figure 8-5 shows an example, already filled in.

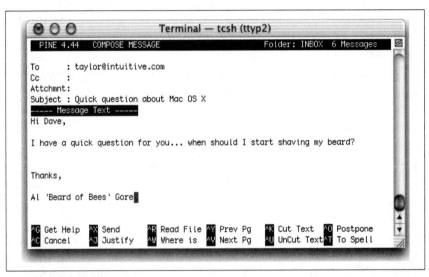

Figure 8-5. Pine composer

As you fill in the header, the composer works differently than when you're in the message text (body of the message). The list of commands at the bottom of the window is a bit different in those cases, too. For instance, while you edit the header, you can attach a file to the end of the message with the "Attach" command, which is Control-J. (Pine uses the ^ symbol to indicate a control character.) However, when you edit the body, you can read a file into the place you're currently editing (as opposed to attaching it) with the

Control-R "Read File" command. But the main difference between editing the body and the header is the way you enter addresses.

If you have more than one address on the same line, separate them with commas (,). Pine will rearrange the addresses so there's just one on each line.

There is more than one way to give the composer the addresses where the message should be sent:

- Type the full email address, for example, *taylor@intuitive.com*.
- Type a nickname from the address book. (See the section "Pine address book" later in this chapter.)

Move up and down between the header lines with Control-N and Control-P, or with the up-arrow and down-arrow keys. When you move into the message body (under the "Message Text" line), type any text you want. Paragraphs are usually separated with single blank lines.

> If you put a file in your home directory named *.signature* (the name starts with a dot, .), the composer automatically adds its contents to the end of every message you compose. (Some other Unix email programs work the same way.) You can make this file with a text editor such as vi, or from the Pine setup menu (see the section "Configuring Pine" later in this chapter). It's good Internet etiquette to keep this file short— no more than four or five lines, if possible.

You can use Pico commands such as Control-J to justify a paragraph and Control-T to check your spelling. When you're done, Control-X (exit) leaves the composer, asking first if you want to send the message you just wrote. Control-C cancels the message, though you'll be asked if you're sure. If you need to quit but don't want to send or cancel, the Control-O command postpones your message; then, the next time you try to start the composer, Pine asks whether you want to continue the postponed composition.

Pine address book

The Pine *address book* can hold peoples' names and addresses, as well as a *nickname* for each person. When you compose a message, enter a nickname in the message header and Pine replaces that with their full name and address.*

---

* The Mac OS X version of Pine also let you store your address book on a central server, in order for you to access it from whatever other computer you're using at the moment, via IMAP.

You can enter information by hand from the main menu by choosing A (address book), then adding new entries and editing old ones. Also, as you read email messages that you've received, the T (take address) command scans the message for email addresses and lets you add them to Pine's address book.

Figure 8-6 shows the address book entry form. Edit each line as you would in the composer, then use Control-X to save the entry. The "Fcc" line gives the name of an optional Pine folder; when you send a message to this address book entry, Pine puts a copy in this folder. (If you leave "Fcc" blank, Pine uses the *sent-mail* folder.) All lines except "Nickname" and "Address" are optional.

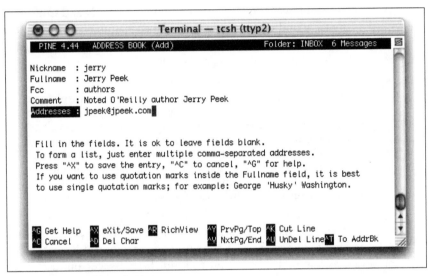

Figure 8-6. Pine address book entry

Once you've saved that address book entry, if you go into the composer and type the nickname *Jerry*, here's the header you get automatically:

```
To      : Jerry Peek <jpeek@jpeek.com>
Cc      :
Fcc     : authors
Attchmnt:
Subject :
```

There's much more to Pine than we can cover here. For instance, it lets you organize mail in multiple folders, print, pipe (output) messages to Unix programs, search for messages, and more.

Exercise: Sending and Reading Mail

You can practice sending and reading mail in this exercise:

Task	Command
Choose a user you know (or choose yourself) and send a short message to that person using pine or your favorite email program.	pine *email-address*
Read the message or messages you got.	pine, or start your favorite email program; use its "read message" commands.
Reply to one of the messages. (It's okay to reply to a message from yourself.)	Press R in pine or use your email program's "reply" command. Send the completed reply.
Forward one of the messages. (It's okay to forward a message to yourself.)	Press F in pine or use your email program's "forward" command. Add a sentence or two of explanation above the forwarded message. Send the completed message.

Usenet News

Usenet, also called "Net News," has thousands of worldwide discussion groups. Each discussion is carried on as a series of messages in its own *newsgroup*. A newsgroup is named for the kind of discussion that happens there. Each message is a lot like an email message. But, instead of being sent to a list of email addresses, a newsgroup message is sent to all the computers that subscribe to that particular newsgroup—and any user with access to that computer can read and reply to the message.

> Because Usenet is a public forum, you'll find a variety of people with a variety of opinions—some impolite, rude, or worse. Although most users are friendly and helpful, a few people seem to cause most of the problems. Until you're accustomed to Usenet, be aware that you may be offended by some contributors and attacked ("flamed") by others.

To read Usenet groups, you'll need a *newsreader* program, also called a *news client*. Many email programs can read news, too. You can use any newsreader; the principles of all are about the same. Some of the more popular Unix newsreaders are slrn, nn, and trn. We show how to read news with Pine Version 4. If you haven't used Pine before, please read the section "Reading Email with Pine" earlier in this chapter.

To set up your copy of Pine to read Usenet messages, go to the Config menu (see "Configuring Pine," earlier in this chapter) and set *nntp-server* to your ISP's or company's news server. You will need to get the name of this server from your ISP or system administrator.

When you choose the L key ("folder list") from the main menu, you'll get a Collection List screen, as shown in Figure 8-7. A *collection* is a group of folders. A collection can be email folders from your local computer, email folders from other computers, or Usenet newsgroup folders. Figure 8-7 shows two collections: *Mail* and *News on news.east.cox.net/nntp*. The news collection is selected (highlighted).

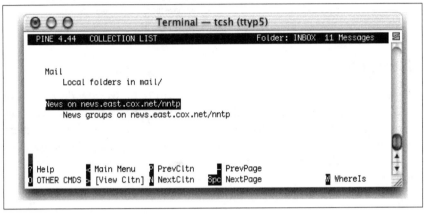

Figure 8-7. Pine Collection List screen

When you press Return or > to view that collection, you'll get a list of newsgroup folders. If your News collection is empty, it means you have not subscribed to any newsgroups. Press A to add a newsgroup. You can either type the name of a newsgroup if you know it, or you can press Control-T to get a list of all newsgroups (press E when you have selected a newsgroup from the list). If you are on a slow link (such as a 56k modem), it could take a long time to get a complete list.

Usenet has something for everyone! The Pine D command will delete a newsgroup from your list; it won't appear anymore unless you use the A command to add it back. (Pine also has some advanced features, such as "zooming" to a list of folders that you've defined. See the Pine help system for details.) Figure 8-8 shows a list of newsgroups.

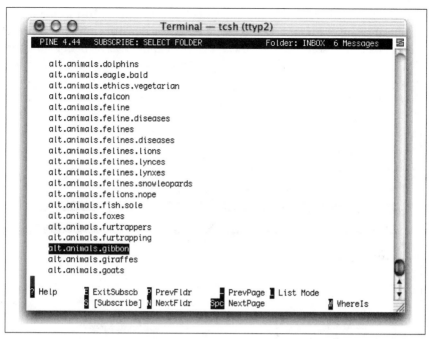

```
● ● ●                  Terminal — tcsh (ttyp2)
PINE 4.44   SUBSCRIBE: SELECT FOLDER           Folder: INBOX  6 Messages

    alt.animals.dolphins
    alt.animals.eagle.bald
    alt.animals.ethics.vegetarian
    alt.animals.falcon
    alt.animals.feline
    alt.animals.feline.diseases
    alt.animals.felines
    alt.animals.felines.diseases
    alt.animals.felines.lions
    alt.animals.felines.lynces
    alt.animals.felines.lynxes
    alt.animals.felines.snowleopards
    alt.animals.felions.nope
    alt.animals.fish.sole
    alt.animals.foxes
    alt.animals.furtrappers
    alt.animals.furtrapping
    alt.animals.gibbon
    alt.animals.giraffes
    alt.animals.goats

? Help        ExitSubscb    PrevFldr       PrevPage  List Mode
              [Subscribe]   NextFldr   Spc NextPage             WhereIs
```

Figure 8-8. Pine newsgroup collection list screen

Newsgroup names are in a hierarchy, with the levels separated by dots (.):

- The main hierarchies include *comp* (for discussions about computers); organization, city, regional, and national groups (such as *ne* for New England, *uk* for the United Kingdom, and so on); *misc* (miscellaneous); and so on. The *alt* (alternative) hierarchy is for almost anything that doesn't fit in the others.

- All the top levels have subcategories, or second-level categories. For instance, the *comp* category has subcategories *comp.sys*, *comp.unix*, *comp.text*, and so on.

- A second-level category may have third-level categories. For instance, the category *comp.sys* is divided into *comp.sys.mac*, *comp.sys.newton*, and so on.

 When you first start to read Usenet, it's a good idea to spend a couple of hours exploring what's available and what you're interested in, and deleting unwanted newsgroups from your list. The time you spend at first will pay you back later, by letting you go straight to the newsgroups in which you're interested.

People all over the world frequent particular newsgroups. Just as mail folders have email messages, newsgroups have *news articles* (individual messages posted by someone). These messages expire after a period of time.
(That's one reason why a lot of newsgroups appear empty.) Let's look into a
newsgroup. Go to the newsgroup *news.announce.newusers*; scroll through
the folder list by pressing the spacebar, or if you're in a hurry, use the W
(Whereis) command and enter the newsgroup name. Once you've selected
the name from the collection list, press Return or > to view it. You'll see a
list of messages in the group, as in Figure 8-9.

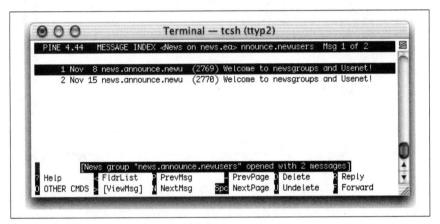

Figure 8-9. Pine newsgroup message index screen

Read Usenet messages just as you read email messages; for example, select a
message from the message index and press Return or > to view it. It stays in
the index until it's deleted or expires. Deleting messages you've read or
don't want to see makes it easier to find new messages that come in later. To
keep a message, save a copy to a Pine mail folder with the S (save) command, email a copy to other users with the F (forward) command, or save a
copy to a file with the E (export) command.

 Remember that people worldwide will see your message and
have your email address. If your message is insulting, long
and rambling, includes a lot of the original message unneces-
sarily, or just makes people unhappy, you're likely to get a
lot of email about it. Many newsgroups have periodic FAQ
(frequently asked questions) postings that give more information about the group and answer common questions. We
suggest that you not post messages to newsgroups until
you've read Usenet for a while, have learned what style is
acceptable, and have seen enough of the discussion in a particular group to know whether your question or comment
has been discussed recently.

If there's a message you want to reply to, the Pine R command starts a reply. After asking whether to include a copy of the original message in your reply, Pine asks you: "Follow-up to newsgroup(s), Reply via email to author or Both?" If you want all who read this newsgroup to see your reply, choose F to follow up; your reply, including your name and email address, is posted for everyone to see. If your message is just for the author—for instance, a question or a comment—replying by email with R is the better choice.

Remember that spammers (people who send "junk email" with advertising and worse) will be able to see the email address on your Usenet posting. For that reason, many people set a different email address in the "From:" field when posting Usenet messages. If your Internet provider gives you multiple email addresses, you could choose one just for your Usenet postings. (Readers may want to reply to your message by email, though, so consider using an email address that you do read occasionally. You also can include your "real" address in the body of the article, possibly disguised to fool spammers who search Usenet articles for email addresses.)

You can post a new message to a newsgroup with the C (compose) command. If you're viewing a news folder, Pine asks if you want to compose a message to that newsgroup. (If you answer N (no), Pine creates a regular email message.)

Here's one more tip: to read expired messages or search through years of archives, web sites such as Google Groups (*http://groups.google.com/*) allow this.

Interactive Chat

Need a quick answer from another user without sending an email message and waiting for his reply? Want to have a conversation with your Internet-connected friend in Chile but don't have money for an international phone call? An interactive chat program lets you type text to another user and see her reply moments later. Chatting, or "instant messaging," has become popular. Widely known chat programs such as iChat, Jabber, and AOL Instant Messenger are available for Mac OS X. Other programs have been available on Unix systems for years and are included with Mac OS X. We look at two of these: talk and IRC.

talk

The talk program is simple to use. Give the username (and, optionally, the hostname) of the person with whom you want to chat. Then talk will try to notify that person as well as show how to use talk to complete the connection with you. Both of your terminal windows will be split into two sections, one for the text you type and the other for the text you get from the other person. You can type messages back and forth until one of you uses Control-C to break the session.

One advantage of talk is its simplicity; if each of you has a terminal window open, either of you can run the program at any time; if the other person is logged in, he is notified that you want to chat and told how to complete the connection. If both people want to use talk on the same computer—even if one of them is logged in remotely (see the section "Remote Logins" in Chapter 7)—it should work well. Unfortunately, there are several talk versions that don't work with each other. So, the first time you try to chat with someone on another host, which might have another talk version (or other problems), it can take planning. Use an email message or phone call to alert them that you'll try talking soon, then experiment to be sure that both of you have compatible talk systems. After that, you're all set.

Here's the syntax:

    talk username@hostname

If the other user is logged onto the same computer as you, omit the @hostname. After you run that command, your screen clears with a line of dashes across the middle. The top half shows text you type and informational messages about the connection. The bottom half shows what the other user types.

For example, if your username is *juan*, you're logged onto the computer *sandya.unm.edu*, and you want to talk to the user *ana* at the computer *cielo.cl*, you would type talk ana@cielo.cl. If the connection works, your screen clears and you'll see something like:

    [No connection yet]
    [Waiting for your party to respond]
    [Waiting for your party to respond]
    [Connection established]
    Hi, Ana! Need any help with your exam?

The message [Waiting for your party to respond] means that your talk program has found *ana*'s system and is waiting for her to respond. Ana's

---

terminal bell should ring and she should see a message like this in one of her terminal windows:

```
Message from Talk_Daemon@sandya.unm.edu at 18:57 ...
talk: connection requested by juan@sandya.unm.edu.
talk: respond with:  talk juan@sandya.unm.edu
```

If she answers by typing talk juan@sandya.unm.edu, the connection should be completed, and her screen should clear and look like yours. What she types appears on the top half of her screen and the bottom half of yours, and vice versa. It's not always easy to know when the other person has finished typing; one convention is to type o (for "over") when you want a response; type oo (for "over and out") when you're finished. The conversation goes on until one person types Control-C to actually break the connection.

Unfortunately, because there are several versions of talk, and because other things can go wrong, you may see other messages from the talk program. One common message is [Checking for invitation on caller's machine], which usually means that you won't be able to connect. If this happens, it's possible that one system has other versions of the talk program that won't work with the particular system to which you're trying to connect—try the ytalk program (available through Fink; see "Fink," earlier in this chapter), for instance. It might also be easier to use a more flexible chat system, such as IRC.

IRC

Internet Relay Chat (IRC) is a long-established system for chatting with other users worldwide. IRC is fairly complex, with some rules you need to understand before using it. We give a brief introduction here; for more details, see *http://www.irchelp.org*. Mac OS X, by default, doesn't include an IRC client, so you'll need to download one. For a good place to start, download the Fink package management system (see "Fink," earlier in this chapter), install it, and then at the Terminal command line type sudo apt-get install ircii to install ircII.

Introducing IRC

Unlike the talk program, IRC programs let you talk with multiple users on multiple channels. Channels have names, usually starting with #, such as *#football*. (You might hope that a channel name would tell you what sort of discussions happen there, but you'd often be wrong!) Many channels are shared between multiple servers on an IRC *net*, or network; you connect your IRC program to a nearby server, which spreads your channel to other servers around the net. Some channel names start with &; these channels are local to their server, and not shared around the net. Finally, you can meet a user from a channel and have a private conversation, a "DCC (Direct Client Connection) chat," that doesn't go through servers.

Each user on a channel has a *nick*, or nickname, which is up to nine characters long. It's a good idea to choose a unique nick. Even when you do, if someone else with the same nick joins a channel before you do, you must choose another nick.

Two kinds of users are in control of each channel. *Ops*, or channel operators, choose which other users can join a channel (by "banning" some users from joining) and which users have to leave (by "kicking off" those users). If a channel is empty, the first user to join it is automatically the channel op. (As you can imagine, this system means that some ops can be arbitrary or unhelpful. If an op treats you badly, though, you can just go join another of the thousands of IRC channels.) *IRC ops*, on the other hand, are technical people in charge of the servers themselves; they don't get involved with "people issues."

IRC not only lets you chat, it lets you share files with other users. This can be helpful, but it also can be dangerous; see the upcoming warning.

There are many IRC programs, or "clients," for different operating systems. They all work with each other, though some have more features. The best known Unix program is ircII, which you run by typing irc. Another well-liked program, based on ircII, is bitchx; get it from *http://www.bitchx.org*. Many programs can be modified by using *scripts* or *bots*; there are thousands of these floating around IRC. But we advise you to use only well-known programs, and to avoid scripts and bots, unless you know that they're safe.

IRC started long before graphical programs were popular. IRC programs use commands that start with a slash (/), such as /join #football or /whois StevieNix. Some IRC programs have buttons and menus that run commands without typing, but you'll probably find that learning the most common commands is easy—and makes chatting faster, overall, than using a mouse.

Finally, you should know that IRC users can get information about you with the /whois *nick* command, where *nick* is your current nick. They'll see your real name unless you set the IRCNAME environment variable to another name in your *.tcshrc* and launch a new Terminal window to make the change take effect. This is explained in the section "Customizing Your Shell Environment" in Chapter 4. (By the way, use /whois with your nick to find out what other people can see about you.)

IRC can be a wide-open security hole if you don't use it carefully. If you type the wrong command or use an insecure program or script, any user can take over your account, delete all your files, and more. Be careful!

IRC programs can be corrupted; scripts and bots can easily do damage. Even if you think that one is widely known and safe, it can contain a few lines of dangerous "trojan horse" code added by an unscrupulous user. Also, never type a command that another IRC user suggests unless you're sure you know what it does; /load and /dcc get can be especially dangerous.

A sample IRC session

When you type irc, your terminal screen splits into two parts. The top part shows what's happening on the server and the channel; the bottom part (a single line) is where you type commands and text. In between the two parts is a status line with the time of day, your nick, and other information. Some terminals can't do what irc wants them to; if you get an error message about this, try the command irc -d to use "dumb mode" instead.

A good ircII command to start with is /help, which provides a list of other commands. The commands /help intro and /help newuser give introductions. For help with a particular command, give its name—such as /help server for help with the /server command. When you're done with help, you'll get a Help? prompt; you can type another help topic name, or simply press Return to leave the help system. Another common command is /motd, the "message of the day," which often explains the server's policies.

You can type your nick on the irc command line. Your IRC program should have a default server. You can change servers with the /server command; you'd do this if your server is full (you get the message "connection timed out," "connection refused," etc.). If your default IRC server is down or busy, you can also give a server hostname on the irc command line, after your nick.

In the following examples, we show the text you type (from the bottom line of the screen) in **boldface**, followed by the responses you might see (from the top of the screen) in unbolded text.

We used these commands:

```
% setenv IRCNAME "Steve St. John"
% irc sstjohn us.undernet.org
*** Connecting to port 6667 of server us.undernet.org
...
*** Closing Link: sstjohn by austin.tx.us.undernet.org (Sorry, your
+connection class is full - try again later or try another server)
```

```
*** Connecting to port 6667 of server us.undernet.org
...
*** Welcome to the Internet Relay Network sstjohn (from
+Arlington.VA.US.Undernet.Org)
...
*** on 1 ca 1(4) ft 10(10)

/motd
*** The message of the day was last changed: 22/12/2001
*** on 1 ca 1(4) ft 10(10)
*** - Arlington.VA.US.Undernet.Org Message of the Day -
*** - 27/7/2001 20:39
...
*** -         SERVER POLICIES:
...

/help newuser
*** Help on newuser
...
*** Hit any key for more, 'q' to quit ***
...
Help? Return

/whois sstjohn
*** sstjohn is ~jpeek@kumquat.jpeek.com (Steve St. John)
*** on irc via server *.undernet.org (The Undernet Underworld)
*** sstjohn has been idle 1 minutes
```

Messages from the server start with ***. Long lines are broken and continue on following lines that start with +. After connecting to the server, we used / whois with our nick to find what information other users could see about us. The Undernet servers have thousands of channels open, so we started by searching for channels with "help" in their names; you can use wildcards, such as *help*, to do this:

```
/list *help*
*** Channel     Users  Topic
*** #helpmania 2      A yellow light, an open door, hello neighbor,
+there's room for more. English
*** #underneth 14     -= UndernetHelp =- Ask your color free questions
+& wait for it to be answered. (undernethelp@fivemile.org)
*** #mIRCHelp  14     Welcome to Undernet's mIRC Help Channel! Beginners
+welcome :-)
*** #irc_help  48     Welcome to #irc_help. We do not assist in
+questions/channels regarding warez, mp3, porn, fserve, etc.
...list goes on and on...

/list *mp3*
...list of groups discussing/sharing MP3 files...
```

We want to see what's happening, so we join the biggest help channel: #irc_help, which has 48 users now:

```
/join #irc_help
*** sstjohn (jpeek@kumquat.jpeek.com) has joined channel #irc_help
*** Topic for #irc_help: Welcome to #irc_help. We do not assist in
+questions/channels regarding warez, mp3, porn, fserve, etc.
*** Users on #irc_help: sstjohn ChuckieCheese Dodgerl GooberZ
+Kinger MotorMouth @theDRJoker MrBean SweetPea LavaBoy GrandapaJoe
...
```

Some names in the list of users, such as *@theDRJoker*, start with @; these users are ops. Let's watch some more of the action. After a couple of users leave the channel, a new user, *MsTiger,* joins and asks for help. Each time a user types a line of text that isn't a command, it's sent to everyone else on the channel, preceded by that user's nick, such as <MsTiger>:

```
*** ChuckieCheese has left channel #irc_help
*** GooberZ has left channel #irc_help
*** HelloWorld (~hw@foo.edu) has joined channel #irc_help
*** MsTiger (~tiger@zz.ro) has joined channel #irc_help
<MsTiger> help me
<MsTiger> please
<Kinger> MsTiger what can we help you with ?
<MsTiger> my channel is not op
<Kinger> LavaBoy tell MsTiger about no opers
<LavaBoy> MsTiger, *shrug*
<GrandapaJoe> MsTiger Sorry, but there are currently NO IRC Operators
+available to help you with your channels. Please be patient and wait
+for an Operator to join.
*** MsTiger has left channel #irc_help
```

The channel has gotten quiet, so we jump in with a question:

```
Hello all.  When I joined, I had a problem
   ...
Any suggestions??
*** Thor (dfdddd@194.999.231.00) has joined channel #irc_help
<[Wizard]> Can you help me plz
<LavaBoy> Try typing !help in the channel, [MORTAL].
/leave
*** sstjohn has left channel #irc_help
/quit
%
```

No one had an answer, so we left the channel after a few minutes of waiting. Other channels might be a lot livelier and might have had someone willing to chat about my question, but we left the irc program by typing /quit. Then we got another shell prompt.

CHAPTER 9
Multitasking

Mac OS X can do many jobs at once, dividing the processor's time between the tasks so quickly that it looks as if everything is running at the same time. This is called *multitasking*.

With a window system, you can have many applications running at the same time, with many windows open. But Mac OS X, like most Unix systems, also lets you run more than one program inside the same terminal. This is called *job control*. It gives some of the benefits of window systems to users who don't have windows. But, even if you're using a window system, you may want to use job control to do several things inside the same terminal window. For instance, you may prefer to do most of your work from one terminal window, instead of covering your desktop with multiple windows.

Why else would you want job control? Suppose you're running a program that will take a long time to process. On a single-task operating system such as MS-DOS, you would enter the command and wait for the system prompt to return, telling you that you could enter a new command. In Unix, however, you can enter new commands in the "foreground" while one or more programs are still running in the "background."

When you enter a command as a background process, the shell prompt reappears immediately so that you can enter a new command. The original program will still run in the background, but you can use the system to do other things during that time. Depending on your system and your shell, you may even be able to log off and let the background process run to completion.

Running a Command in the Background

Running a program as a background process is most often done to free a terminal when you know the program will take a long time to run. It's also used whenever you want to launch a new window program from an existing terminal window—so that you can keep working in the existing terminal, as well as in the new window.

To run a program in the background, add the & character at the end of the command line before you press the Return key. The shell then assigns and displays a process ID number for the program:

```
% sort bigfile > bigfile.sort &
[1] 29890
%
```

(Sorting is a good example because it can take a while to sort huge files, so users often do it in the background.)

The process ID (PID) for this program is 29890. The PID is useful when you want to check the status of a background process, or if you need to cancel it. You don't need to remember the PID, because there are Unix commands (explained in the next section) to check on the processes you have running. Some shells write a status line to your screen when the background process finishes.

In tcsh, you can put an entire sequence of commands separated by semicolons (;) into the background by putting an ampersand at the end of the entire command line. In other shells, enclose the command sequence in parentheses before adding the ampersand. For instance, you might want to sort a file, then print it after sort finishes:

```
(command1; command2) &
```

The examples above work on all shells. Mac OS X Unix shells also have a feature we mentioned earlier called *job control*. You can use *suspend character* (usually Control-Z) to suspend a program running in the foreground. The program pauses, and you get a new shell prompt. You can then do anything else you like, including putting the suspended program into the background using the bg command. The fg command brings a suspended or background process to the foreground.

For example, you might start sort running on a big file, and, after a minute, want to send email. Stop sort, then put it in the background. The shell prints a message, then another shell prompt. Send mail while sort runs.

```
% sort hugefile1 hugefile2 > sorted
...time goes by...
CTRL-Z Stopped
% bg
[1]    sort hugefile1 hugefile2 > sorted &
% pine taylor@intuitive.com
```

Checking on a Process

If a background process takes too long, or you change your mind and want to stop a process, you can check the status of the process and even cancel it.

ps

When you enter the command ps, you can see how long a process has been running, the process ID of the background process, and the terminal from which it was run. The tty program shows the name of the Terminal where it's running; this is especially helpful when you're logged into multiple terminals, as the following code shows:

```
% ps
  PID TT  STAT      TIME COMMAND
  310 std S       0:00.37 -tcsh (tcsh)
  510 std R+      0:00.00 ps
  459 p2  S+      0:00.25 -tcsh (tcsh)
% tty
/dev/ttyp1
```

std corresponds to your current Terminal window, and p2 corresponds to the Terminal window for ttyp2. In its basic form, ps lists the following:

Process ID (PID)
    A unique number assigned by Unix to the process.

Terminal name (TT)
    The Unix name for the terminal from which the process was started.

Run time state (STAT)
    The current state of each job. S is sleeping, R is runnable, T is stopped, and I is idle (sleeping for more than 20–30 seconds). Additionally, the state can include + to indicate it's part of the foreground group process, E to indicate the process is exiting, and W to mean it's swapped out.*

Run time (TIME)
    The amount of computer time (in minutes and seconds) that the process has used.

COMMAND
    The name of the process.

Each terminal window has its own terminal name. The previous code shows processes running on two windows: *std* and *p2*. If you want to see the processes that a certain user is running, type ps -U *username*, where *username* is the username of someone logged into the system.

---

* The ps manpage has details on all possible states for a process. It's quite interesting reading.

To see all processes running on the system, use ps -ax. The -a option shows processes from all users, and the -x option shows processes that are not connected with a Terminal session; many of these are processes that are a core part of Mac OS X, while others may be graphical programs you are running, such as a web browser.

Watching System Processes

ps -ax tells you what system processes are running, but if you want to see what they are up to, you'll need to look in the system log. To view the system log, use the command tail. It's kind of like cat, except that it only prints the last few lines of the file. If you use the -f option, it will follow the file as it grows. So, if you open up a new Terminal window and issue the following command, you can monitor the informational messages that come out of system utilities:

```
% tail -f /var/log/system.log
Nov 20 08:39:42 Itchy xinetd[368]: Started working: 1 available
service
Nov 20 08:39:42 Itchy ConsoleMessage: Starting Apache web server
Nov 20 08:39:43 Itchy mach_kernel: IP packet filtering initialized,
divert enabled, rule-based forwarding enabled, default to accept,
logging disabled
Nov 20 08:39:43 Itchy mach_kernel: IP firewall loaded
```

You can also see some system messages by running the Console application (*/Applications/Utilities*).

You can also specify process ID values to ps to find out about specific jobs. Consider the following:

```
% sort verybigfile > big-sorted-output
[1]  522
% ps 522
  PID TT  STAT      TIME COMMAND
  522 std R      0:00.32 sort verybigfile
% ps $$
  PID TT  STAT      TIME COMMAND
  310 std S      0:00.41 -tcsh (tcsh)
```

As the last command shows, you can easily ascertain what command shell you're running at any time by using the $$ shortcut for the process ID of the current shell. Feed that to ps, and it'll tell you about the shell process you're running.

You should be aware that there are two types of programs on Unix systems: *directly executable programs* and *interpreted programs*. Directly executable programs are written in a programming language such as C and have been compiled into a binary format that the system can execute directly. Interpreted programs, such as shell scripts and Perl scripts, are sequences of commands that are read by an interpreter program. If you execute an interpreted program, you will see an additional command (such as perl, sh, or csh) in the ps listing, as well as any Unix commands that the interpreter is executing currently.

Shells with job control have a command called jobs that lists background processes started from that shell. As mentioned earlier, there are commands to change the foreground/background status of jobs. There are other job control commands as well. See the references in the section "Documentation" in Chapter 10.

Canceling a Process

You may decide that you shouldn't have put a process in the background or the process is taking too long to execute. You can cancel a background process if you know its process ID.

kill

The kill command terminates a process. This has the same result as using the Finder's Force Quit command. The kill command's format is:

    kill PID(s)

kill terminates the designated process IDs (shown under the PID heading in the ps listing). If you do not know the process ID, do a ps first to display the status of your processes.

In the following example, the sleep *n* command simply causes a process to "go to sleep" for *n* seconds. We enter two commands, sleep and who, on the same line, as a background process.

```
% (sleep 60; who)&
[1] 543
% ps
  PID TT STAT     TIME COMMAND
  310 std S     0:00.52 -tcsh (tcsh)
  543 std S     0:00.00 -tcsh (tcsh)
  544 std S     0:00.01 sleep 60
  545 std R+    0:00.00 ps
  459 p2  S+    0:00.25 -tcsh (tcsh)
% kill 544
# Terminated
taylor    console  Feb  6 08:02
```

```
taylor    ttyp1    Feb  6 08:30
taylor    ttyp2    Feb  6 08:32
```

[1]   Done   (sleep 60; who)

We decided that 60 seconds was too long to wait for the output of who. The ps listing showed that sleep had the process ID number 544, so we use this PID to kill the sleep process. You should see a message like "terminated" or "killed"; if you don't, use another ps command to be sure the process has been killed.

In our example, the who program is now executed immediately, as it is no longer waiting on sleep; it lists the users logged into the system.

Problem checklist

The process didn't die when I told it to.

Some processes can be hard to kill. If a normal kill of these processes is not working, enter kill -9 *PID*. This is a sure kill and can destroy almost anything, including the shell that is interpreting it.

In addition, if you've run an interpreted program (such as a shell script), you may not be able to kill all dependent processes by killing the interpreter process that got it all started; you may need to kill them individually. However, killing a process that is feeding data into a pipe generally kills any processes receiving that data.

CHAPTER 10

Where to Go from Here

Now that you're almost to the end of this guide, let's look at some ways to continue learning about the Unix side of Mac OS X. Documentation is an obvious choice, but it isn't always in obvious places. You can save time by taking advantage of other shell features—aliases, functions, and scripts—that let you shorten a repetitive job and "let the computer do the dirty work."

We'll close by seeing how you can use Unix commands on non-Unix systems.

Documentation

You might want to know the options to the programs we've introduced and get more information about them and the many other Unix programs. You're now ready to consult your system's documentation and other resources.

The man Command

Different versions of Unix have adapted Unix documentation in different ways. Almost all Unix systems have documentation derived from a manual originally called the *Unix Programmer's Manual*. The manual has numbered sections; each section is a collection of manual pages, often called manpages; each program has its own manpage. Section 1 has manpages for general Unix programs such as who and ls.

Mac OS X has individual manpages stored on the computer; users can read them online. If you want to know the correct syntax for entering a command or the particular features of a program, enter the command man and the name of the command. The syntax is:

```
man command
```

For example, if you want to find information about the program vi, which allows you to edit files, enter:

```
% man vi
.
.
%
```

The output of man is filtered through a pager in Mac OS X like less or more automatically.

After you enter the command, the screen fills with text. Press the spacebar or Return to read more, and q to quit.

Mac OS X also includes a command called apropos or man -k to help you locate a command if you have an idea of what it does but are not sure of its correct name. Enter apropos followed by a descriptive word; you'll get a list of commands that might help. To get this working, however, you need to first build the apropos database. This is done when Mac OS X runs its weekly maintenance job, which can be run manually with the following command:

```
% sudo periodic weekly
Password:
%
```

Now you can use apropos to find all commands related to PostScript, for example, with:

```
% man -k postscript
enscript(1)           - convert text files to PostScript
grops(1)              - PostScript driver for groff
pfbtops(1)            - translate a PostScript font in .pfb format to
ASCII
```

Problem checklist

man says there is no manual entry for the command.

Some commands—cd and jobs, for example—aren't separate Unix programs; they're part of the shell. On Mac OS X, you'll find documentation for those commands in the manual page for tcsh.

If the program isn't a standard part of your Unix system—that is, your system staff added the program to your system—there may not be a manual page, or you may have to configure the man program to find the local manpage files. The third possibility is that you don't have all the manpage directories in your MANPATH variable. If so, add the following to your *.tcshrc* (see "Creating and Editing Files" in Chapter 3), then open a new Terminal window for the settings to take effect:

```
% setenv MANPATH /sw/share/man:/sw/man:${MANPATH}:/usr/X11R6/man
```

Documentation via the Internet

The Internet changes so quickly that any list of online Unix documentation we'd give you would soon be out of date. Still, the Internet is a great place to find out about Unix systems. Remember that there are many different versions of Unix, so some documentation you find may not be completely right for you. Also, some information you'll find may be far too technical for your needs (many computer professionals use and discuss Unix). But don't be discouraged! Once you've found a site with the general kind of information you need, you can probably come back later for more.

The premier place to start your exploration of online documentation for Mac OS X Unix is the Apple web site. But don't start on their home page. Start either on their Mac OS X page (*http://www.apple.com/macosx/*) or their Darwin project home page (*http://developer.apple.com/darwin/*). Another excellent place to get information about software downloads and add-ons to your Unix world is the Fink project (see "Fink" in Chapter 8).

Many Unix command names are plain English words, which can make searching hard. If you're looking for collections of Unix information, try searching for the Unix program named grep. One especially Unix-friendly search engine is Google, at *http://www.google.com*. Google offers a specialized Macintosh search engine at *http://www.google.com/mac* and a BSD search engine at *http://www.google.com/bsd* (which is useful because Mac OS X's Unix personality derives from its BSD heritage).

Here are some other places to try:

Magazines
Some print and online magazines have Unix tutorials and links to more information. Macintosh magazines include MacTech (*http://www.mactech.com*), MacWorld (*http://www.macworld.com*), and MacAddict (*http://www.macaddict.com*).

Publishers
Those such as O'Reilly & Associates, Inc. (*http://www.oreilly.com*), have areas of their web sites that feature Unix and have articles written by their books' authors. They may also have books online (such as the O'Reilly Safari service) available for a small monthly fee—which is a good way to learn a lot quickly without needing to buy a paper copy of a huge book, most of which you might not need.

Universities
Many schools use Unix-like systems and will have online documentation. You'll probably have better luck at the Computer Services division

(which services the whole campus) than at the Computer Science department (which may be more technical).

Mac OS X–related web sites

Many Mac OS X web sites are worthy of note, though they're run by third parties and may change by the time you read this. Mac OS X Apps (*http://www.macosxapps.com*) offers a wide variety of Aqua applications. Information on Darwin can be found at Open Darwin (*http://www.opendarwin.org*), and Mac OS X Hints (*http://www.macosxhints.com*) offers valuable information and hints. One more site well worth a bookmark is O'Reilly's MacDevCenter (*http://www.macdevcenter.com/*).

User Groups

Apple User Groups are an excellent source of information, inspiration, and camaraderie. To find an Apple User Group near you, see *http://www.apple.com/usergroups/*.

Books

Bookstores, both traditional and online, are full of computer books. The books are written for a wide variety of needs and backgrounds. Unfortunately, many books are rushed to press, written by authors with minimal Unix experience, full of errors. Before you buy a book, read through parts of it. Does the style (brief or lots of detail, chatty and friendly or organized as a reference) fit your needs? Search the Internet for reviews; online bookstores may have readers' comments on file.

Shell Aliases and Functions

If you type command names that are hard for you to remember, or command lines that seem too long, you'll want to learn about *shell aliases* and *shell functions*. These shell features let you abbreviate commands, command lines, and long series of commands. In most cases, you can replace them with a single word or a word and a few arguments. For example, one of the long pipelines (see the section "Pipes and Filters" in Chapter 6) could be replaced by an alias or function named (for instance, aug). When you type aug at a shell prompt, the shell would list files modified in August, sorted by size.

Making an alias or function is almost as simple as typing in the command line or lines that you want to run. References in the section "Documentation" earlier in this chapter, have more information. Shell aliases and functions are actually a simple case of shell programming. For more information on aliases, see "Creating Aliases" in Chapter 4.

Programming

We mention earlier that the shell is the system's command interpreter. It reads each command line you enter at your terminal and performs the operation that you call for. Your shell is chosen when your account is set up.

The shell is just an ordinary program that can be called by a Unix command. However, it contains some features (such as variables, control structures, and so on) that make it similar to a programming language. You can save a series of shell commands in a file, called a *shell script*, to accomplish specialized functions.

Programming the shell should be attempted only when you are reasonably confident in your ability to use Unix commands. Unix is quite a powerful tool and its capabilities become more apparent when you try your hand at shell programming.

Take time to learn the basics. Then, when you're faced with a new task, take time to browse through references to find programs or options that will help you get the job done more easily. Once you've done that, learn how to build shell scripts so that you never have to type a complicated command sequence more than once.

You might also want to learn Perl or Python. Like the shell, Perl and Python interpret script files full of commands. But these two programming languages have a steeper learning curve than the shell. Also, because you've already learned a fair amount about the shell and Unix commands by reading this book, you're almost ready to start writing shell scripts now; on the other hand, a programming language will take longer to learn. But if you have sophisticated needs, learning one of these languages is another way to use even more of the power of your Unix system.

Glossary

alphanumeric

Characters: letters (*alpha*) and numbers (*numeric*), including punctuation characters (such as _ and ?).

AppleTalk

A suite of transport protocols first introduced in Mac OS 7 and included in all systems since that release. One advantage of AppleTalk is that it's very easy to add and modify devices on an AppleTalk network.

Aqua

The graphical appearance of Mac OS X.

BSD

The Berkeley Software Distribution version of Unix, BSD was the academic Unix, compared to System V, from AT&T Bell Telephone Labs, which had more of a commercial bent.

command

An instruction that you can give to a program running on the Unix system. For instance, you can type a program's name and arguments on a command line, at a shell prompt; this command asks the shell to run that program. (The shell is a program itself; see *shell*.) Once a program starts running, it may accept commands of its own. For example, a text editor has commands for deleting and adding text to the file it's editing.

The terms *command* and *program* are used almost interchangeably, probably because the program name is typed first on a command line (at a shell prompt). Shells have some *built-in* commands that don't start a separate program running; one of these is cd, which changes the shell's working directory.

cracker

A malicious person who tries to break into computer systems (usually via a network), disrupt computers and networks, steal secrets (such as passwords and credit card numbers), and exhibit other antisocial behavior.

Popular media often call these people *hackers*. But, to most computer people, a hacker is someone who enjoys computing and programming, and may be an expert at some area of it. (For instance, a *Perl hacker* is someone who's good at programming in the Perl language.)

Darwin

A hybrid of Mach (an operating system from Carnegie-Mellon University) and BSD Unix that serves as the underpinnings of Mac OS X (with the addition of many other Mac OS X technologies such as Aqua).

Desktop

The part of a display that's "behind" (not enclosed within) the windows, icons, and other items on the display.

directory

Also known as a *folder*. A list of files and/or other directories. A directory is actually a special kind of file that has names and locations of other files and directories. See also *working directory*.

Finder

A graphical filesystem browser for your Macintosh. Prior to Mac OS X, the only way you could interact with your system was through the Finder, but now you can also opt to use the Terminal.

Fink

A group of volunteers who test, fix, and package open source software so it runs on Mac OS X. See *http://fink.sourceforge.net/*.

FreeBSD

An open source operating system based on the original BSD Unix. Darwin derives some features from FreeBSD. See *http://www.freebsd.org/*.

Free Software Foundation (FSF)

An organization formed in 1985 that works for the rights of computer users to study, copy, modify, and redistribute computer programs. The FSF also distributes free software. See *http://www.fsf.org/*; see also *GNU*.

GNU

A project, started in 1984, to develop a completely free Unix-like operating system: the GNU system. GNU stands for "GNU's Not Unix;" it is pronounced "guh-NEW." See also *Free Software Foundation*.

multitasking

An operating system that can run more than one program at a time is said to be a *multitasking OS*. On single-processor Macs, the programs don't actually all run simultaneously; the OS can divide the computer's time between the different programs very rapidly, so that they all *appear* to run at the same time. The system can still be overloaded and run slowly, if too many programs are trying to run at once.

Unix has always been multitasking, and Macintosh systems have been multitasking for many years too.

NetBSD

An open source operating system based on the original BSD Unix. Darwin derives some features from NetBSD. See *http://www.netbsd.org/*.

pathname

The location of a file or directory in a Unix filesystem: a series of names separated by slash (/) characters. Pathnames can be *absolute* (starting with a slash character, which means they begin at the filesystem's root directory) or *relative* (not starting with a slash, which means the pathname starts from the current working directory). See also the section "The Mac OS X Filesystem" in Chapter 2.

process

A program that's been loaded into memory and has started executing. It has a state associated with it (such as running, suspended, or sleeping), and has a portion of memory allocated to it.

program

A set of instructions to the computer, written by a programmer, and stored in a file. The program is executed when you type its name as the first word on a command line, at a shell prompt (or when you choose the program from a menu or icon in a window system). Unix runs a program as a *process*, which you can suspend or terminate using job control, an interrupt key, or the `kill` command.

root (user and directory)

Unix systems have an account named *root*, also called the "superuser," that has no protections or restrictions. System administrators and staff use this account to make changes to the system's configuration and operation. Mac OS X users can access this account with `sudo` (see "Superuser Privileges with sudo" in Chapter 2).

A Unix filesystem is like an upside-down tree with a branching structure of directories inside directories. The first directory, where the filesystem starts, is called the *root directory*.

screen

The area of a terminal (usually glass or plastic) that shows computer output. See also *terminal*.

session

When two programs, or two users running programs, communicate across a network, they typically start the communication by doing a certain thing—for instance, by logging in. The communication continues until it's completed (or, possibly, aborted before it completes)—for instance, by logging out. The entire process, from start to completion, is called a *session*.

shell

A program that runs other programs. There are several different kinds of shells, each with its own command-line syntax; Mac OS X uses *tcsh* as the default, but others are available including *bash* and *zsh*. All shells do the same basic job: read commands that you type interactively at a shell prompt or read

commands noninteractively from a program file called a *shell script*.

When you start using Terminal, a shell program begins to run and prints a shell prompt. When you terminate that shell (by typing `exit` or Control-D at a prompt), you're logged out from that Terminal.

syntax

The rules for, or the format of, the characters you use to make a command or other computer input. For example, the syntax of a Unix command line is explained in the section "Syntax of Unix Command Lines" in Chapter 1.

working directory

When you give Unix a *relative* pathname to a file or subdirectory, the working directory is the starting point—the directory where that relative pathname starts. For example, if your working directory is */Users/joe/food* and you type the command `less recipes/fish`, Unix opens the file */Users/joe/food/recipes/fish*. (Your working directory is still */Users/joe/food*.)

If you type the command `ls ..` from any working directory, you get a listing of the files in your parent directory. That command uses the relative pathname to the parent directory (..). So if your working directory is */Users/joe/food*, that command would list the parent directory */Users/joe*. Or, if your working directory is */Users/joe*, that same command would list the parent directory */Users*.

Each process running on a Unix system has its own working directory, which the program can change at any time. For instance, you can give the shell the command `cd` to change its working directory.

Index

We'd like to hear your suggestions for improving our indexes. Send email to *index@oreilly.com*.

B

background processes, 6, 118, 120
BBEdit text editor, 39
bg program, 119
bitchx program, 114
bots, 114
BSD (Berkeley Software
       Distribution), 129
buffer, 58

C

C (Config) command, 100
cat command, 74
cd command, 17
channel operators (Ops), 114
characters, alphanumeric, 129
chat programs, 111–117
chgrp command, 31
chmod command, 28
    permissions arguments, 28
chown command, 32
CMD (Command), 120
collections (Pine), 108
comma (,) and Pine, multiple email
       addresses, 105
Command (CMD), 120
command line, 3
    editing, 5
    syntax, 7–9
command-line FTP, 89–91
command-line interfaces, ix
commands, 129
    ⌘-. (canceling commands), 5
    ⌘-~ (switch window), 2
    ⌘-C (command interrupt or
           cancel), 5, 6
    ⌘-D (end of input command), 6
        filename matches, listing with, 24
    ⌘-E (use selection for find), 2
    ⌘-F (find in scroll buffer), 2
    ⌘-G (find next), 2
    ⌘-H (erase character), 5
    ⌘-J (jump to selection), 2
    ⌘-N (open Terminal window), 2
    apropos, 125
    apt-get utility, 94–96
    atprint, 71
    background, running in, 118–119
    canceling, 5, 6

cat, 74
cd, 17
chgrp, 31
chmod, 28
chown, 32
close terminal (exit), 6
Control-Q (resume output), 6
Control-S (pause output), 6
Control-U (erase command line), 6
Control-Z (suspend program
       operation), 119
cp (see cp command)
CpMac program, 49
curl, 91
date, 4
df, 24
du, 23
end input (⌘-D), 6
enscript, 68
erase character (⌘-H), 5
erasing the command line (⌘-U), 6
find, 50
fink install, 95
fink list, 96
grep, 78
kill, 122
less, 25–26, 80
locate, 51
lpq, 70
lpr, 69
lprm, 70
ls, 19–23
m2u, 40
man, 124
mkdir, 46
mv, 49
MvMac, 50
noclobber, 75
open Terminal window (⌘-N), 2
pause output (⌘-S), 6
Pine utility (see Pine)
pr, 66
ps, 120
ps2pdf, 72
pwd, 17
recalling previous, 5
resume output (⌘-Q), 6
rm, 51
rmdir, 52
rsh, 86

About the Authors

Dave Taylor is a popular writer, teacher, and speaker focused on business and technology issues. He is the founder of The Internet Mall and *iTrack.com* and has been involved with Unix and the Internet since 1980, having created the popular Elm mail system. He's also been a Mac fan since their original release, when he started out with a dirty beige Mac Plus. Previous positions include being a research scientist at HP Laboratories and senior reviews editor of *SunWorld* magazine. He has contributed software to the official 4.4 release of Berkeley Unix (BSD), and his programs are found in all versions of Linux and other popular Unix variants.

Brian Jepson maintains a keen focus on the sparks that fly where two cutting edges meet. Mac OS X is one such intersection, combining a sold Unix core with the pioneering Apple user interface. Brian's prior experience developing applications in Unix and Linux gives him an appreciation of the target audience's point of view. His thorough explorations of NeXTSTEP and Mac OS X—conducted over the last few years—kept him oriented as he developed this book. Brian is also an O'Reilly editor and co-author of *Mac OS X for Unix Geeks*.

Colophon

Our look is the result of reader comments, our own experimentation, and feedback from distribution channels. Distinctive covers complement our distinctive approach to technical topics, breathing personality and life into potentially dry subjects.

The animal on the cover of *Learning Unix for Mac OS X*, Second Edition, is an Alaskan malamute. The Alaskan malamute is one of the oldest Arctic sled dogs. These powerful dogs have muscular bodies, structured for strength and endurance. They have broad heads with bulky muzzles and triangular ears, which stand erect to signify alertness. Their thick coats are coarse and dark on the outside, with soft, woolly undercoats.

Alaskan malamutes make excellent companions, as they are affectionate, friendly, and loyal. They can be playful, but tend to become more reserved as they mature. They are very intelligent, with eyes that reveal their curiosity and interest.

Jane Ellin was the production editor and proofreader for *Learning Unix for Mac OS X*, Second Edition. Brian Jepson and Sheryl Avruch provided quality control. Joe Wizda and John Bickelhaupt wrote the index.

Emma Colby designed the cover of this book, based on a series design by Edie Freedman. The cover image is an illustration from the *Illustrated Natural History: Mammalia*. Emma Colby produced the cover layout with QuarkXPress 4.1 using Adobe's ITC Garamond font.

David Futato designed the interior layout. This book was converted to FrameMaker 5.5.6 with a format conversion tool created by Erik Ray, Jason McIntosh, Neil Walls, and Mike Sierra that uses Perl and XML technologies. The text font is Linotype Birka; the heading font is Adobe Myriad Condensed; and the code font is LucasFont's TheSans Mono Condensed. The illustrations that appear in the book were produced by Robert Romano and Jessamyn Read using Macromedia FreeHand 9 and Adobe Photoshop 6. The tip and warning icons were drawn by Christopher Bing. This colophon was written by Linley Dolby.

Want To Know More About Mac OS X?

The Apple Developer Connection offers convenient and timely support for all your Mac OS X development needs.

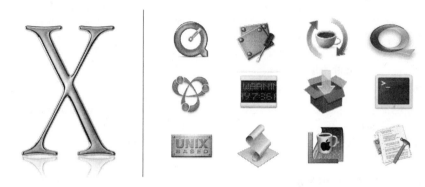

Developer Programs

The Apple Developer Connection (ADC) helps developers build, test, and distribute software products for Mac OS X. ADC Programs provide direct, affordable access to Mac OS X software, along with many other products and services, including:

- Pre-release software seeds
- Apple hardware discounts
- Code-level technical support

Programs range in price from $0 (free) to US$3500 and are available worldwide.

Developer Tools

All ADC Program members receive free Mac OS X Developer Tools such as Project Builder, Interface Builder, and Apple-Script Studio.

Getting Started is Easy

The ADC web site offers a variety of reference materials including in-depth articles, tutorials, sample code, and FAQs. You'll also find student developer resources, open source projects, mailing lists, and more. Our electronic newsletter keeps members notified with up-to-the-minute information on new releases and documentation.

Join today!
Visit http://developer.apple.com/ membership/

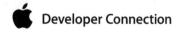

How to stay in touch with O'Reilly

1. Visit our award-winning web site

http://www.oreilly.com/

★ "Top 100 Sites on the Web"—PC Magazine
★ CIO Magazine's Web Business 50 Awards

Our web site contains a library of comprehensive product information (including book excerpts and tables of contents), downloadable software, background articles, interviews with technology leaders, links to relevant sites, book cover art, and more. File us in your bookmarks or favorites!

2. Join our email mailing lists

Sign up to get email announcements of new books and conferences, special offers, and O'Reilly Network technology newsletters at:

http://elists.oreilly.com

It's easy to customize your free elists subscription so you'll get exactly the O'Reilly news you want.

3. Get examples from our books

To find example files for a book, go to:

http://www.oreilly.com/catalog

select the book, and follow the "Examples" link.

4. Work with us

Check out our web site for current employment opportunites:

http://jobs.oreilly.com/

5. Register your book

Register your book at:
http://register.oreilly.com

6. Contact us

O'Reilly & Associates, Inc.
1005 Gravenstein Hwy North
Sebastopol, CA 95472 USA
TEL: 707-827-7000 or 800-998-9938
       (6am to 5pm PST)
FAX: 707-829-0104

order@oreilly.com
For answers to problems regarding your order or our products. To place a book order online visit:

http://www.oreilly.com/order_new/

catalog@oreilly.com
To request a copy of our latest catalog.

booktech@oreilly.com
For book content technical questions or corrections.

corporate@oreilly.com
For educational, library, government, and corporate sales.

proposals@oreilly.com
To submit new book proposals to our editors and product managers.

international@oreilly.com
For information about our international distributors or translation queries. For a list of our distributors outside of North America check out:

http://international.oreilly.com/distributors.html

adoption@oreilly.com
For information about academic use of O'Reilly books, visit:

http://academic.oreilly.com

O'REILLY®